breeding
budgerigars

cessa feyerabend
and
dr. matthew m. vriends

ISBN 0-87666-970-4

Distributed in the U.S. by T.F.H. Publications, Inc., 211 West Sylvania Avenue, P.O. Box 427, Neptune, N.J. 07753; in England by T.F.H. (Gt. Britain) Ltd., 13 Nutley Lane, Reigate, Surrey; in Canada to the book store and library trade by Clarke, Irwin & Company, Clarwin House, 791 St. Clair Avenue West, Toronto 10, Ontario; in Canada to the pet trade by Rolf C. Hagen Ltd., 3225 Sartelon Street, Montreal 382, Quebec; in Southeast Asia by Y.W. Ong, 9 Lorong 36 Geylang, Singapore 14; in Australia and the South Pacific by Pet Imports Pty. Ltd., P.O. Box 149, Brookvale 2100, N.S.W., Australia; in South Africa by Valiant Publishers (Pty.) Ltd., P.O. Box 78236, Sandton City, 2146, South Africa; Published by T.F.H. Publications, Inc., Ltd., The British Crown Colony of Hong Kong.

Contents

This lithograph is the earliest known picture of a budgerigar.
It was drawn by Dr. Lear and lithographed by Nodder in 1805.

I. Breeding Budgerigars

History

The native land of the budgerigar is Australia where great numbers of this small parrakeet rove the plains and fill the air with their melodious, warbling, song-like chatter. The color of the wild budgerigar is grass green with a yellow mask adorned with three black spots on either side. The wing markings are black and yellow, the arrangement of which gives a wavy appearance. Each little black feather is edged with yellow, resembling small shells. Hence, the name "shell parrakeet" was given to this species.

The naturalists Shaw and Nodder were the first to describe the budgerigar (in 1805) and give it the Latin name *Melopsittacus undulatus*. A full, detailed description of this bird was published by the famous naturalist John Gould, who studied and recorded the bird life of Australia. John Gould brought the first four live specimens to England in 1840.

The name budgerigar was derived from *betcher-rygar* or *boodgereegar* or similar names, variously spelled, which were used by the natives of Australia and mean "good food" or "pretty bird." In this country the name *parrakeet* or *lovebird* is still being used though these terms have proved rather confusing. The true lovebird does not belong to the parrakeet family; he is a short-tailed African bird that differs greatly from the budgerigar. The name parrakeet denotes the group and not the species.

There are more than a hundred species of parakeets*, distributed all over the tropical zone. Some of these have been captured and by patient tutoring have

---

* To readily differentiate the extreme differences among the members of the large parakeet family, the editors spell the names of the larger species with a single r; the names of species of the Shell and Grass group with a double r.

learned to repeat quite a number of words and sentences. Chief among these are the Ringnecked Parakeets and the Alexandrine Parakeets which were imported from India and neighboring islands. Today many other species of the large parakeet group are bred in captivity, but none has proved as hardy and prolific as the budgerigar.

Budgerigars are a migratory species and are seen here and there throughout the interior of Australia. Great numbers will breed in a certain location one year and be conspicuous by their absence the following season. Swarms consisting of tens of thousands may pass by overhead and not be seen again for several years. In years when seeding grasses are scarce, little breeding goes on and the nests are small. In years when food is plentiful, the bush is alive with breeding budgerigars, and the large eucalyptus trees and dead tree stumps of the White-Gum tree and Mallee (a low-growing eucalyptus) all bear several nest hollows, most containing three to four young. The average number of eggs is six.

Budgerigars are seldom seen in the coastal region but appear at times in almost any part of the Australian interior, except the narrow strip of moving dunes in the center. They feed on grass seeds, are known to visit water holes regularly, and are fond of rolling in dew-wet grass, which is their manner of taking a bath. Though they can get along without water for a few days, it is a mistake to believe that they do not need water or an opportunity to bathe.

The northern part of Australia is in the tropical zone. There is a general belief that the tropics are hot and humid. This is not always true, for the tropical region of Australia lies in the hot arid (dry) belt. In this region, the temperature rarely drops below sixty-five degrees F. during even the coolest month, which is July. The hottest month is January with an average temperature of about eighty degrees. During hot spells daytime peaks may reach occasionally 120 degrees.

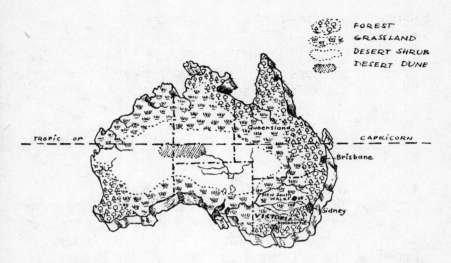

FOREST
GRASSLAND
DESERT SHRUB
DESERT DUNE

The continent of Australia. Wild budgerigars roam through the grassland and desert shrub regions. They are not found in either the wooded and coastal regions or the central desert dunes.

The nights are twelve hours long and cool.

In the Australian interior, vegetation sprouts quickly after tropical rains, and budgerigars lose no time raising nests of young in such localities, regardless of the time of year. Their molting season is as erratic as their breeding season. In this respect they are true tropical birds. Feathers are shed sporadically just as tropical trees shed their leaves at irregular times and not during a definite season.

In the southeastern part of Australia, New South Wales, and occasionally northern Victoria, wild budgerigars breed during the Australian spring. This region lies in the south temperate zone. The humidity is very low and, though on rare occasions the temperature rises to 106 degrees during a short mid-day period, the average temperature ranges around seventy degrees since the nights are long and cool. The climate is a delightful one.

At the beginning of the Australian summer (December), budgerigars cease breeding and begin travelling north into the tropical zone. There may be several reasons for this, among them the fact that vegetation dries up, the bird population has increased, and food becomes scarce in the southeastern nesting territory. In Queensland, budgerigars are known to breed in June (winter in Australia). In the interior and northwest parts, where it is not too hot, they breed during any month of the year.

Early Years in Captivity

Budgerigars have been bred in Europe since 1840. Shiploads of wild green birds of this species were captured in Australia and imported. About 1880 the largest breeding farms were built in southern France. In Toulouse, as early as 1888, M. Bastide had nearly 20,000 budgerigars, and by 1913 the establishment covered two and a half acres of ground and housed about 100,000 budgerigars. Needless to say, the feather disease French Molt, as well as numerous breeding troubles, took their toll under these conditions of mass production.

Budgerigar breeding in the United States started early in the twentieth century, California leading the way with the first large establishments.

Present-day Breeding in America

This book was written for those who love birds and who want to breed choice specimens of good physique, good health, and exquisite type and color. The question, "When is the best season for breeding budgerigars?" is discussed periodically in current bird publications and views of experienced American breeders are found to differ from those in other countries.

Winter Breeding

Budgerigar breeders on other continents have often wondered why breeders in Great Britain are so much

8

This Opaline Cinnamon hen is a beautiful young bird. The arrival of this variety in the late 1930's created a sensation in the fancy.

opposed to winter breeding. British fanciers recommend that budgerigars be bred in spring and summer only. Many ailments, including French Molt, are attributed to breeding these birds during the winter months. Fresh greens, so necessary in the breeding season, are now available all winter because of modern transportation. It may help to understand the reasons for this prejudice in Britain against winter breeding if we consult a map of the world.

Australia, which is the native habitat of the budgerigar, is relatively close to the equator and consequently daylight hours do not have much seasonal variation. Even the northern areas of the United States lie closer to the equator than England.

The shortest day in Britain is five and three-quarter hours in the north and seven and three-quarter hours in the south, while the shortest day in New York is over nine hours. The longest day in the northern, tropical zone of Australia is about thirteen hours; the shortest day about ten and one-half hours. The southern part of Australia, in the south temperate zone, has a daylight hour range from nine and one-half to fourteen hours.

Budgerigars are not seasonal breeders, so seasonal instincts are not involved. In Australia these birds travel from their southern breeding grounds to the north and breed there again, in spite of the fact that summer days are shorter in North Australia than in the south. This shows that budgerigars do not come into breeding condition with lengthening daylight hours as seasonal breeders do. Why then have British fanciers always advised against breeding these birds in winter?

The answer lies in a combination of sleep and nutrition, both influenced by the number of hours of natural daylight. Most birds are extremely sensitive to the change from day to night. They want to rise with the sun and go to sleep at sunset. Budgerigars, according to close observation, react this way to the change of

An aviary for budgies must be damp-proof and draft-proof, yet there must be ample fresh air and correct ventilation.

day and night natural to the region in which they live. Winter days in Britain are, therefore, too short for breeding budgerigars successfully, while winter days in the United States are longer and no ill effects have been noticed. Turning on lights in indoor breeding establishments in the northern part of the United States at sundown and letting them burn for approximately one hour during the shortest days of the year (December to January) will be of benefit. This small increase has not noticeably harmed the birds, but a longer time of light hours beyond natural day length definitely upsets them and does not bring about a longer feeding period. Crops have been found to be full of food at sundown. When kept up too long, birds will be sleepy during the day and feeding of young will suffer. Those breeders who are in favor of artificial light late in the evening are of the opinion that this benefits the birds because they have observed that the parents feed their young at that time. Budgerigars feed their young

These aviaries face south, giving ample provision for sunlight, and the overhanging vegetation provides shade.

at regular intervals during the night even when it is completely dark. We have observed that unnaturally long hours of light do not cause the young to grow larger nor is general production increased. In fact the young usually are smaller and hens display signs of nervousness. Budgerigars are well equipped to store enough food in their capacious crops to feed their young through winter nights in the United States. Outdoor breeding establishments in the southern states do not need artificial light at any time during the year.

To summarize, winter breeding in the United States may be considered quite safe, while winter breeding in Britain is not recommended. There seems to be no reason, however, why budgerigars in England should not be set up for breeding by the end of January if artificial heat is supplied. Days will be long enough for successful raising of young by the time they have hatched.

Budgerigars will breed outdoors at temperatures

below freezing, but growth of the young is seriously retarded in cold weather and hens may become egg-bound from chill. For breeding purposes a temperature fluctuating in this way is better than a steady one. Non-breeding budgerigars are not harmed by temperatures of twenty to twenty-five degrees Fahrenheit if kept in spacious aviaries where there is plenty of flight room, a protected shelter and abundant food.

Spring Breeding
Spring is the ideal breeding season in the United States, except in the humid southeast where late spring may become too hot.

Summer Breeding
The value of the summer months for breeding budgerigars has been debated by fanciers. England has moderate summer temperatures, but in the United States summer is not a favorable breeding season for budgerigars because, except in desert country and at high altitudes, the atmosphere is too humid in hot weather. Temperatures in Australia during the day are often high, but the air is dry and the nights are cool and long. But even in Australia budgerigars rarely breed in extremely hot weather and, if they do, it is only for one nest. Nesting holes do not get as overheated there as they do here.

In captivity, breeding in summer may be carried out successfully if, by insulating, drying, or air conditioning, temperature and humidity can be kept down. If no protection against high humidity can be provided, budgerigars should not be bred in July and August. In the humid southern United States, especially in the southeastern portion, breeding activities should come to an end in May.

Fall Breeding
The fall of the year is considered unfavorable by

some budgerigar breeders. In Britain fall days soon become too short, but this is not true in the United States and there seems no reason why fall should not be a good breeding season. Some fanciers on the North American continent claim that fall-raised birds are not as good as spring-raised ones. We have raised some of our best and largest budgerigars in the fall.

Breeders who send birds to bird shows do not breed their best birds in fall because bird shows take place during the autumn and exhibition specimens are not mated until the shows are over. Those who breed their poorer specimens in the autumn should realize that this is the explanation for the inferiority of their fall-bred birds.

Some breeders think that one disadvantage of raising budgerigars in autumn, in places where the winters are cold, is that young birds cannot be turned out into open air flights for growth and development. They have to be kept indoors until early spring, whereas spring-bred birds receive great benefit from growing up outdoors in natural sunlight.

However, by feeding cod-liver oil to birds in indoor flights excellent results in raising young budgerigars have been achieved. Many breeders never turn out their birds into the open air, yet some of the best birds in the country have been raised in such aviaries. Many aviaries in locations where budgerigars can be kept outdoors all the year round have not raised as good birds as those produced by indoor breeding establishments. It would seem that good care and management are the decisive factors, rather than outdoor flights.

One argument used by breeders who do not favor fall breeding is that the birds have not finished molting. This is an erroneous statement. We know that budgerigars are tropical birds and do not have a definite molting season. While some of the birds are not in complete feather, others are. Those sent to bird shows are not molting. Of course, it is necessary at all times to

Some fanciers let their budgerigars remain in the open flights no matter what the weather is like, whereas many others believe that snow and frost can not be beneficial to a budgie's health.

select only breeding birds which are in good feather and good condition. It is also necessary to give indoor stock proper hours of lighting. If lights are kept on much beyond natural daylight hours for that time of year, inferior birds will be raised in autumn. It is a great mistake to supply spring day hours of light during the shorter fall days. It is best always to adhere as closely as possible to natural conditions.

Sex Characteristics

It is of primary importance, when starting to breed birds, to obtain true breeding pairs. One should be a

15

male, the other a female. This may seem to be an unnecessary statement, but too often "pairs" have been sold to a novice which consist of two hens or two cocks.

The sex of a mature budgerigar is easily distinguished. Adult birds have a waxy skin around their nostrils, called the cere, which is of a rich blue color in the male and whitish, tan, or brown in the female. These sex

Soon after the birds have left the nest, it is usually easy to distinguish the cocks from the hens. The cocks have blue ceres (also called "wattles"), whereas the hens' ceres are brown. Shown here is a hen.

characteristics do not become apparent until the age of about six months. Some of the birds mature earlier. This may be due to environmental causes, that is, care, housing, lighting, and feeding, or it may be due to hereditary causes. There are birds of certain strains which, when kept under the same conditions with other birds, always mature earlier than birds from the other strains. Some birds grow their adult coat of feathers early and develop the mature color of their cere late or vice versa.

We like to see a rough brown cere in hens of breeding age and in good breeding condition. However, some hens never develop a deeply colored cere even if they have attained breeding age and are in good general health. The cere remains tan or light brown, yet such hens breed well and raise good young. On the other hand, some young hens only six to eight months old show a smooth brown cere. Breeders may be tempted to breed such hens, but it is inadvisable to force such birds into breeding too early. A hen with a white cere should not be bred because a white cere, which occasionally shows bluish edges, may mean the hen is not in breeding condition or may be in ill health. There are a few exceptions.

Mature cocks display a blue cere of rich color all the year around. When cocks are not healthy, this color usually fades. Moreover, running noses resulting from colds or disease tend to discolor the cere.

Sex characteristics of immature budgerigars are not pronounced. The cere shows an indefinite whitish, bluish, or fleshy tone. Sometimes it is blue at the edges. With beginning maturity young hens develop a slight tan coloring at the center of the cere, the bluish tinge gradually disappears while the tan spreads, until finally the whole cere deepens to the rich brown color of the mature hen.

Baby budgerigars of both sexes may easily be distinguished from adult birds by their coat of feathers. Adult budgerigars have a yellow or white forehead, while in young budgerigars the striated feathers of the head and neck extend down to the cere. This is particularly noticeable in the darker colors such as greens and blues. Yellows and whites do not show this distinction clearly. All baby birds have a rather flat head and their body feathers are of a dull appearance. The black wing markings of the adult bird are of a brownish color in the baby bird, and the breast color is fainter or of a slightly different shade.

The eyes of baby budgerigars look different from

those of adult birds. The colored part, the iris, is deep brown in young birds and cannot be distinguished by the naked eye from the black center, the pupil. With approaching maturity the iris changes to a lighter color until it is a clear yellow in the normal adult budgerigar. The exceptions, of course, are the red or ruby-eyed varieties.

Between the ages of three and five months, young budgerigars lose their nest feathers and begin to grow adult feathers. White and blue budgerigars begin to sprout white pinfeathers above the beak. Gradually, males commence to show the high, rounded, white forehead, while females show a white, less rounded forehead. On green or yellow budgerigars the new feathers of the forehead will be yellow.

Sex of immature budgerigars is not always easy to tell. Some breeders have the knack of being able to spot a young cock that is still in the nest by behavior (untamed hens in the nest bite harder than baby cocks) and by the pinkish color of the cere. Others can detect minute differences in the shape of the cere. The Japanese are adept at telling sex in young birds by their "look-see" method. They examine the shape of the vent.

A safe method of sexing budgerigars while still in the nest is to mate a cock of one of the sex-linked varieties (such as Opalines or Cinnamons) to a normal hen. The cocks in the nest will be split to the sex-linked variety, but will look like normal cocks. All the young hens will show the color of the sex-linked variety and thus can be distinguished easily from the cocks. Difficulties in sexing will be experienced with the Lutinos, Fallows, Albinos, etc.

Occasionally an old hen which has had her yellow or white forehead for some time will show again on her forehead the black striations of the baby bird. This does not mean that such a bird will not breed. This peculiarity has not been explained, but it seems to have no influence on breeding behavior.

A beautiful Cinnamon hen. In the Cinnamon Green series the mask and ground color of the wings have to be yellow, but in the Cinnamon or Skyblue (as in Fallows, Cobalts, Mauves, etc.) series, clear white is required on the wings and the mask.

Breeding Condition

The factors which constitute breeding condition in budgerigars differ considerably from those found in birds which are seasonal breeders. In the case of the latter, healthy specimens will automatically come into breeding condition when the proper season approaches. In the case of budgerigars, other factors must be considered.

1. **Breeding Age.** There are many differences of opinion among budgerigar fanciers about various phases of budgerigar breeding, but one point on which all experienced breeders agree is the minimum age at which these birds should be allowed to start nesting activities. The accumulated wisdom of a hundred years lies behind the statement that budgerigars should not be allowed to breed until at least one year old.

Some hens look fully mature at the age of six months and are often sold as mature breeders at that age. Young raised from immature breeding stock will not come up to the standards set by first-class budgerigar breeders. Budgerigars are not fully grown and mature until about one year old. As a matter of fact, they still grow and broaden out a little during their second year of life.

As a protection against buying immature stock, which is sometimes sold as mature by unscrupulous people, the purchaser of breeding stock should ask for birds wearing closed leg bands. Among other marks of identification these bands bear the year when the birds hatched. Any reliable breeder or pet shop will gladly furnish the month of birth with each bird sold.

Unfortunately, budgerigars are prolific breeders. Young hens barely three months old and still in their baby feathers have been known to go to nest and rear young. Needless to say, such precocity will soon run down the strain. Diseases like French Molt, bad feathering, bald spots, vices, etc., will spread among the flock and it will become more and more unprofitable. Any infectious disease which might be introduced will find good material for a rapid spread. It is important, therefore, to remove young budgerigars from quarters which are equipped with nest boxes, particularly where mature cocks may be ready and eager to pick up a mate.

Some breeders believe that it is best not to use budgerigars for breeding until two years old. This procedure may bring good results occasionally, but as a rule it is best to allow birds to breed when they have attained full maturity. In most cases there seems to be no advantage in waiting overly long before providing them with a mate and facilities for breeding.

The maximum age at which budgerigars may be bred varies considerably. A hen may be a satisfactory breeder for eight or ten years if she has not been bred until one year old, if she has not been allowed to raise more than two nests a year with not more than four young to a nest, if she has always received the best of care and if she has remained healthy. Denys Weston, English authority on budgerigars for a long period of years, wrote an interesting item on "Cage Birds" stating that he never used a hen above twelve years of age for breeding. He does not advise using hens as old as this. He then states that a cock had been a good breeder to the age of twenty-seven years and was then sold with a guarantee for fertility. The purchaser later informed Mr. Weston that the cock had proved a good breeder and had sired winners. We have seen a cock that raised his last nest of young and then dropped dead at the age of nineteen years. We have also had experience with cocks that became sterile at the age of six or eight years. Heredity and care play a big role and no definite statement can be made as to how long budgerigars should be kept for breeding. Some hens begin to produce small young after five years of age. Hens of poor stock with bad heredity or hens which have been overbred and underfed will cease to produce good young after two years.

It is doubtful whether hens that have not been used

Nest boxes can be made of various patterns, but it is preferable not to have them less than 6 inches x 5 inches by 8 inches. All bottoms should be removable; the concave portion of each bottom should be about three-quarters of an inch deep in the center. As budgies like to perch in the nest opening, it is necessary to have some ventilation holes in the sides of the box, just under the roof.

for breeding every year will retain the ability to raise good young for more years than those that have raised a limited number of young every year.

2. Health and Feather. Health is as important as age in the selection of breeding stock. How can we tell which birds are in good breeding condition? After making sure that our birds have had a rest period of at least six months since raising their last batch of young, we should see that they are in perfect health and good feather. They should be entirely through with the molt, should be bright and alert, wear their feathers smoothly, have bright eyes and deeply colored ceres. Dull birds with rough plumage and missing long feathers should never be used for breeding.

Among seasonal breeders, hens show their desire to

breed with the lengthening of daylight hours. They are seen picking up threads or twigs in preparation for nest building. Budgerigar hens display obvious signs of wanting to breed only when they see suitable nesting places such as nest boxes, when courted by a lively cock, and when in company with birds of their species. In selecting hens for the breeding room the above factors should be considered. Although some hens may show the desire to breed in an obvious form, most do not. Breeding condition simply means that the hens should be rested and in good health and feather.

It must be remembered that budgerigars are very sociable and it is indeed an exception when a solitary pair begins to breed. Wild budgerigars breed in large colonies. In captivity two or three pairs should be set for breeding with cages so placed that the birds can see the other pairs in neighboring cages.

Being non-seasonal breeders, intensity of light is of slight importance. These birds have often been taken in from sunny outdoor flights into breeding rooms with a much lower supply of light and still have started to go to nest promptly. Attention should be paid, however, to the number of hours of light the birds were used to before being placed into breeding quarters. Any sudden change will upset them and the desire to breed will be delayed until they have adapted themselves to the different lighting regime. Slightly shortened hours of light will not do as much harm as a sudden big increase. It should always be kept in mind that the best hours of light are from sunrise to sunset and the birds should be gradually accustomed to these hours.

Not all budgerigars come into breeding condition at the same time. We cannot decide by the calendar when to put up our birds for breeding. We have to select those which are ready, allowing others more time in the flight until they, too, have finished molting completely and are lively and ready for the arduous task of raising young.

Life in the Breeding Cage

Before breeding pairs are introduced into breeding cages, everything should be ready for them. Each breeding cage contains one nest box and houses one pair.

The period of preliminary courting varies widely. Sometimes the cock will begin courting immediately or within a few hours, sometimes not until several days have passed.

When there is a complete lack of mutual interest over a period of weeks, the breeder should look for causes of this abnormal behavior. The birds may have been raised under unfavorable conditions or suffer from dietary deficiencies. If there are no signs of ill health, it is possible that the problem is one of adjustment to new conditions. If cocks and hens have been kept in the same flight, they have selected their own mates during the pre-breeding period and will refuse to accept mates selected by the breeder. Hens are particularly finicky in this respect. Even when transferred from one aviary to another in the same locality, birds often feel strange. They are not used to their new owner and his manner of caring for them and are, therefore, disturbed and likely to go out of breeding condition. The period of light may be different from what the birds were used to. The hens may lose the brown of their cere and require some time before returning to breeding condition. The new owner may be too anxious about his birds, constantly watch them, peek into the nest boxes, show them to friends, etc. The breeder should make sure that mites, mice, dogs, cats, or children do not disturb or harass the birds.

After a period of investigation, the hen disappears into the nest box for longer and longer periods. She may spend most of her time in it for about a week before laying. At night, however, she will sleep outside. Sometimes the birds hang on the wires during the night. They often select what seem to us most uncomfortable positions while sleeping. Many an inex-

24

perienced owner has forced his budgerigars to sit properly on a perch for the night, thus upsetting the birds and delaying breeding activities.

Most hens pull small body feathers from their breast to line the nest and to thin their coat of feathers. Their own body heat will then contact the eggs better during incubation. Small feathers in the nest, therefore, should not be confused with a molt which is discussed in the book "Diseases of Budgerigars " (T.F.H. Publ. Inc., Neptune, N.J.).

When the cock has fertilized the hen, eggs will eventually arrive. At this time it is important not to disturb the pair. A hen getting ready to lay is very sensitive to disturbance. Thorough cleaning of the cage should be postponed until several eggs have been laid. It frequently happens that an extended cleaning job while a young hen is laying has upset her so much that eggs are dropped on the floor, or the hen stops laying after only one or two eggs. In such a case more eggs were probably on the way but were reabsorbed. Much time will be lost until the hen again produces eggs. With young hens it may happen that eggs are dropped on the cage floor without apparent reason. If not broken or cracked, they may cautiously be put into the nest box. The hen may or may not accept them. Most hens will soon get straightened out and lay their eggs in the nest box.

Budgerigars usually lay in the afternoon. After the first one or two eggs have been laid, the hen will remain in the nest box most of the time, especially during the night. Her cloaca becomes relaxed allowing excrement to accumulate. When leaving the nest box on rare occasions, she will discharge excrement of an entirely different nature from that dropped at other times. It will be very large and soft.

Most cocks do not enter the nest box during incubation of the eggs. This is the sole duty of the hen. However, an occasional cock will enter the nest box and join the hen in incubating the eggs. They will sit on the eggs side by side, the cock facing one way, the hen the other.

One egg is laid every other day. If the hen has been incubating from the first day, the first egg will hatch two days before the second one and so on. If the hen has not been sitting constantly on the first egg, there may be only one day difference in hatching time. Occasionally the first two eggs will hatch the same day. The average size of the first clutch of eggs if five or six; up to eleven or twelve have been reported in later clutches. The period of incubation lasts from seventeen to twenty days, depending on the temperature of the breeding room and the moisture content of the air. In a warm room (between sixty-five and seventy degrees Fahrenheit) the embryos will grow faster within the

The hen lays one egg every other day. The number of eggs in each clutch varies from three to ten, with five or six being the most usual number. A one-day-old youngster is shown next to an egg in this photo.

egg. Their growth is somewhat delayed at a cooler temperature. The incubation period of budgerigars is never less than seventeen days. Normally, one chick hatches from one egg, but the hatching of twins from one large egg has been reported.

Great joy follows hatching of the first chick. Hatching usually takes place in the early morning hours, but may happen during the day. The proud owner will hear the small voice of the newly hatched chick during the first day. On peeking into the nest box he will see a tiny, reddish creature with large closed eyes and no feathers or down of any kind. The two halves of the empty shell will still be lying on the side of the nest, unless the mother has already removed them. The new chick's parents seem as proud of their offspring as the owner. The mother caresses her baby and the father frequently peeks into the nest box at feeding time. The father feeds the mother and the mother feeds the young.

The remaining eggs will hatch in due time. When five eggs have hatched, the oldest chick will be eight days older then the youngest. Newly hatched chicks grow extremely fast. Many inexperienced breeders worry that the youngest, being so much smaller than its older brothers and sisters, will not be fed or will be trampled on and die. This rarely occurs. Death of young chicks in the nest has a number of other causes which are discussed in the books on nutrition and diseases*. Some breeders, who have young hatching simultaneously in a number of nests, exchange them in such a way that each nest will contain young of the same age. Although the parents rarely object to this procedure, it interferes with the natural feeding habits of the budgerigar and will call for some complicated adjustments which should be avoided. This sort of interference may in some cases precipitate addiction to vices in the birds.

* "Modern Feeding of Budgeriars" and "Diseases of Budgerigars" (T.F.H. Publ. Inc., Neptune, N.J.).

However, if the first three chicks of, let us say, eight eggs, have hatched and the next four eggs did not hatch, the chick hatching from the eighth egg will be so much smaller than its older brothers and sisters, that it is advisable to take this last chick out of the nest and transfer it to a nest containing young of its size. It will hardly have a chance to survive otherwise.

Feeding of Young

The method by which the budgerigar hen feeds her young is most interesting and deserves special attention. The young are fed with a substance regurgitated from the crop called budgie milk. Little is known about the anatomy and physiology of the budgerigar crop, except that it has much in common with the crop of the pigeon. For instance, the pigeon also produces a milk-like substance used in feeding young. We may, therefore, draw on information regarding the pigeon's crop which extends from the esophagus (gullet) as two

Note the size differential between the two-day-old budgies (bottom of photo) and the eight-day-old chick at the top.

When the young hatch it is essential to look into the boxes more often to ring the young, remove bad eggs or dead chicks and change the bedding to keep the nest boxes clean.

pocket-like bags. The inner lining consists of layers of cells while the pigeons are incubating eggs. These cells contain much fat and are rich in proteins. As soon as the young hatch, the cells break away from the crop lining, mix with mucus from the mucous glands, and are regurgitated as a milk-like curd with which the mate and the young are fed. It may be that some digestive juices are forced up from the stomach and mix with the crop contents, but there are no glands in the crop secreting digestive juices. It serves as a storage organ and the seeds are softened therein.

Newly hatched budgies do not receive any seeds during the first few days of their lives. Their crop after feeding contains a yellowish liquid which can be squeezed out. Food in the crop of the hen undergoes a separation of liquid and solid matter. The budgerigar hen feeds the youngest chick first. It receives the most liquid part of the crop contents. When the chicks are several days old, a few seeds are found in their liquid crop contents. As the chicks grow, more seeds are

29

found in the crop along with bits of green stuff. It is amazing to see, in a nest of five, that the crop of each chick contains a different proportion of solids and liquids. The crop of the youngest holds nothing but liquid while that of the oldest is crammed with seeds. This proves that the budgerigar hen knows how to feed young of varying ages and it is, therefore, inadvisable to exchange young in order that all the babies in one nest be the same size.

Not only during the day, but also through the night, the tiny voices of the young may be heard now and then while being fed. The mother feeds her newly hatched babies about four times an hour. The intervals become longer as the young grow larger. As their crops grow in capacity more food can be taken in with each feeding. Small babies are fed while lying on their backs. As they get larger and stronger they begin to sit up and stretch their necks out to the mother. She regurgitates the food from her crop and feeds them in the same way as the cock feeds her. The mother hen's crop dilates during the period of feeding young. At sundown it is filled to capacity with food and is visible as a large bulge.

It is of great importance to have a liberal supply of seeds and grit in the breeding cages at all times while birds are feeding their young. Fresh greens must be supplied daily. Clean water is equally important as the cocks especially drink a great deal of water while young are in the nest. It aids in the formation of "budgie milk."

The Young

While the babies are small, the mother keeps them covered and warm, at the same time incubating the remaining eggs. The young cuddle together in a little heap, resting their long necks on one another. After a few days their eyes begin to open. This is a slow process, only a little slit of the black pupil shows at first, widening gradually with each day. They are homely little creatures before their feathers have grown, but in about one week the down begins to show and eventually covers the whole chick with a warm, woolly coat. At two weeks the bird's color can be seen by observing the sprouting tail feathers.

When feathers begin to grow on the babies, the mother ceases to cover them and sleeps outside the nest box at night. An interesting phenomenon appears at this time. When the young hear any unusual sound, especially during the night, they break out in a chorus

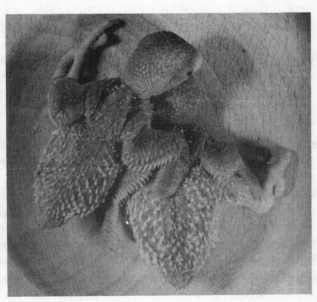

The two budgies shown here are about eleven days old. As the budgies are hatched on different days, they do not all leave the nest box simultaneously.

of unbelievably loud chatter for such small creatures. Their beaks are wide open, their tongues move up and down, and their lungs are evidently strained to capacity. It must be that natural enemies are intended to be scared off by this noise. After all, the young at this time are unprotected in the nest cavity and unable to escape an enemy which might approach through the nest hole. We should think that a weasel or other marauder hearing this tremendous clatter, would not suspect a group of tiny helpless birds in the nest, but an enemy considerably larger and more ferocious than itself and would flee at great speed from this dangerous site.

When the head feathers are still very short, the beaks are prominent, giving the birds the appearance of small eagles. The beaks are deep blackish brown in color, which begins to fade when the birds leave the nest. A trace is often still visible until the age of five or six weeks but soon disappears completely. At three weeks the breast feathers begin to open and reveal their color.

The young budgerigar at the age it emerges from the nest box fully feathered is a beautiful little creature. It is clean and fluffy with large black eyes (except the red-eyed varieties). The young budgie's first step is to climb up to the nest hole from the inside to take a look at the outside world. It seems that the hen stops feeding a baby when it reaches a certain size. Hunger drives the baby bird up to the nest hole where it loudly voices its desire for food. This is where the cock steps in. He comes to the nest hole and feeds the baby, filling up its empty crop. Soon the next oldest realizes where it can obtain food for its ever hungry stomach. Gradually the babies will emerge from the nest box, not necessarily the oldest one first. Often the first-hatched stays inside until several young leave the nest together for a short period of the day. Now the cock has full charge of the brood, while the hen takes care of the last babies in the nest or incubates a new clutch of eggs. She does feed the young outside occasionally when she happens to be off the nest.

During the first days outside the nest box the young receive vigorous training from both parents. They are constantly hungry, eternally begging for food, but nine times out of ten they are refused attention. Instead they are purposely pushed from the perches so that they fall down to the cage bottom where food may be found. Often a youngster begging too hard is chased around the cage for some time by an exasperated parent. It is then forced to find its own food morsels. However, the parents, mainly the cock, will feed the young sometimes, especially toward evening when crops must be filled for the night. The young usually return to the nest box for the night if bred in cages.

Budgerigars bred in cages leave the nest box sooner than those bred in large aviaries, where nest boxes are high on the walls and inaccessible to a baby bird not yet able to fly. In spacious breeding pens no youngster leaves the nest until it can fly well.

The principal reason for a hen turning out her young is that she has started laying her second clutch of eggs and resents interference while laying and incubating. Some hens at this stage will not allow the young to return to the nest box at all. They refuse them entrance, but do not injure them. An occasional hen becomes so exasperated with young bobbing in and out of the nest box that she attacks them, often wounding them on the head. Sometimes she is driven into such a rage that she pursues the offending youngster and mutilates it so severely that death occurs, or the horrified owner has to put the injured young bird out of its misery. Such extreme nervousness and tendency to cannibalism in hens is often due to nutritional deficiencies and overbreeding. When vicious habits in the hen are noticed, the young must be removed to different nests.

Other hens are more tolerant and seem to believe in self-expression for their offspring. Young of the first clutch are allowed to go in and out of the nest box as much as they like, with the result that some eggs of the second clutch are ruined from being soiled and milled around by the young of the first clutch. These unfortunate occurrences are not the rule. In most cases the second clutch of eggs is larger than the first and a sufficient number of young will hatch.

The breeder of show stock prefers to leave the young

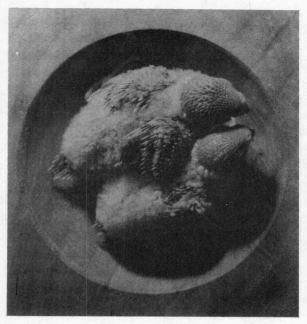

These budgies are about sixteen days old. When feathers begin to grow on the babies, the mother ceases to cover them and sleeps outside the nest box at night.

with the parents as long as they still receive an occasional feeding, thus insuring maximum growth. Babies removed at the earliest moment possible, though they feed themselves, often do not eat enough food at this period and do not grow as large as those receiving supplementary feedings from the parents while learning to eat.

One method of inducing young to eat by themselves early is to put a tablespoon of canary seed and oatmeal into the nest box daily when the oldest have reached the age of three and one-half weeks. When young are leaving the nest, a flat dish of seeds containing a larger portion of canary seeds should be placed on the cage floor within easy reach. At first the babies may not be able to find the regular seed hopper.

At about the age of six weeks, when the young birds are seen to eat alone, they should be removed from the breeding cage. Most breeders find it expedient to give them another week or two in a large cage before turning the young birds out into the flights.

When the young of the second clutch are beginning to leave the nest, the third clutch of eggs is laid; but a pair of budgerigars should not be allowed to raise three nests of young in one season. Two nests are enough to take from a pair. Laying eggs and feeding young saps the strength of the parent birds. Breeders who want to raise good, healthy birds always destroy the third clutch of eggs. The young of the third clutch often do not turn out well and the parent birds may become so exhausted that they will not raise healthy young the following year.

Some breeders, to avoid the laying of a third clutch of eggs, remove the nest box while the young of the second clutch are still very small. They place the young in a box on the cage floor where they will be fed by the parents. The hen, without a nest box, may drop one or two eggs on the cage floor but will then stop laying. Others take the cock out, leaving the nest box in its

The babies pictured here are about twenty-three days old. At this age the feathers begin to open and reveal their color.

Below: Almost fully fledged, this month-old baby budgie will soon leave the nest. **Opposite:** This sturdy, very heavy bird was raised as a lone chick. The "lone chick" system of raising only one baby from each clutch is going out of favor among the big exhibitors, who feel that some of the giants are getting coarse.

place, but this does not always keep the hen from laying. Or the hen is taken out, leaving the cock to care for the young. However, not all cocks are good feeders. Personally, we prefer to leave both parents with their young and destroy the third clutch of eggs. Parents feed better when their home life is not disturbed and they feed the young in the nest box better than those outside. It is advisable, therefore, to leave the box in its place so the young may return to it and keep warm. The young grow better and stronger when properly protected while small.

Those breeders who are interested only in quantity production allow their budgerigars to raise nest after nest. One pair of which we have knowledge has raised ninety-four young in succession. This is a remarkable example of fecundity. However, the breeder who owned this pair has given up raising budgies. All his birds developed French Molt and ceased to breed properly.

Removal of One Parent

Occasionally it becomes necessary to take one of the parents out of the breeding cage while young are in the nest. The cock or the hen may become ill, or the hen may become a severe feather plucker. It can also happen that the hen takes a sudden dislike to her mate, attacks him and nearly kills him. In this case, to save the unfortunate cock's life, he must be removed from the breeding cage. In our aviaries we have had only one hen so far which attacked the cock with murderous intent while young were in the nest. The cock had contracted a bad cold from a draft. He suffered from diarrhea and evidently his digestion had become upset. We noticed that the young had caked food around the outside of their beaks ("Dirty Feeders"). If, as seems likely, the hen's sudden dislike of the cock was caused by his supplying her and indirectly her young with unwholesome food, then she showed great intelligence. After the cock was removed, she successfully finished feeding her clutch of young alone. In other cases, if the hen has to be taken out of the breeding cage, the cock will feed the young alone.

Although hens are regarded as the more dangerous, occasionally a cock may also become murderous. One of our cocks attacked his hen each time the babies were old enough to begin leaving the nest. He would follow her into the nest box and nearly scalp her. The hen in turn became so nervous that she attacked the young after they left the nest. This cock fought with several hens in the same manner. Previous to the breeding season there were some furious fights in the cock flight and we suspect that this same cock was the instigator, because the fights stopped after he had been removed to a breeding cage.

Hens, as a rule, are good feeders and take care of their young even if the cock has to be removed. Cocks need some watching if left alone with young which are still quite small. It is best in such a case to transfer some young to another nest, if possible, and allow the cock to feed not more than two or, at the most, three young. A little before sundown the crops of the young should be examined. If they are well filled, the cock has proved to be a good feeder. If the crops are empty or only partially filled, the young will have to be transferred or hand-fed.

Foster Parents

Budgerigars, if healthy and of good stock and receiving sensible care, are good feeders of their young. Nevertheless, some kind of difficulty may arise to necessitate the transfer of young from one nest to another. For this purpose some breeding pairs are used to raise young other than their own. These are called foster parents and have often saved valuable chicks that would have perished without them. Foster parents are also used to raise chicks from parents which are rare or first class show birds and are not allowed to

Sometimes the male and female parents in a pair of breeding budgies have to be separated from each other to prevent damage caused by fighting. Although the hen (far left) and cock (second from left) pictured here show a little wear and tear after their second nest, they generally got along very well and produced some prize-winning youngsters.

raise young themselves. (If it is decided to allow such a pair to raise only two young, the rest should be transferred.)

The transfer of eggs or young demands special consideration. Breeding birds have a strict rhythm and their instinctive behavior is closely bound to it. This means that foster hens should lay at the same time as the pairs whose young they are going to raise. A novice breeder who has been told that budgerigars will gladly feed strange young may make the mistake of putting young birds into a nest where the hen is just beginning to lay. At this time she will not tolerate such interference. She is not ready to care for young at this phase. In most cases she will proceed to murder the little strangers which were put into her nest box.

The best time for transfer is after the young have been banded. A record kept on the birds will always identify them. If the transfer has to be made before closed leg bands can be put on, the breeder will have to make sure he can identify the young offspring of a certain pair by some other means. Identification may be made if the young grow feathers of a different color from that of the foster parents, or they may be much older, or much younger, than the babies whose nest box they have come to share. However, if they are only a little smaller or a little bigger than the other young in the nest, they may be hard to identify when banding time comes. Young do not always grow at an even rate. A small bird, after a few days, may look as large or larger than one which was bigger at the time of transfer. To forestall the possibility of any mistake, a brush mark of vegetable dye can be used on the chick as a means of identification if it must be transferred before banding.

Transfer is preferably done in the forenoon after the chicks have had their morning feeding, but about one hour before sundown the crops of the transferred chicks should be checked. If crops are not well filled, the chicks have to be returned to their original nest.

Partway through the second round, the hen begins to look a little worn. A pair of budgies should not be allowed to rear more than two clutches of youngsters per season. It is advisable to change youngsters from one pair of parents to another to produce uniformity in size and numbers. Budgerigars are very co-operative in this matter and do not object when other parents' babies are offered to them.

This is rarely necessary, however, if the chicks do not differ too greatly in size from the ones in the foster nest. Needless to say there should not be more than four or five young in a nest.

The transfer of eggs is simple if all eggs of the foster parents are destroyed, but if some remain the eggs which are added have to be marked. A dab with a vegetable dye such as is used for cooking purposes will identify them. Even then it is difficult at times to be certain of the parentage of chicks in the same nest. Transfer of young is preferable to transfer of eggs.

It is not advisable to keep birds of inferior quality for the purpose of raising foster chicks. Plans do not always work out according to a rigid schedule and the young of the inferior birds might be raised because none of the valuable stock were available for transfer at the right time.

Banding

For pedigreed stock it is necessary to slip closed leg bands on birds at the age of about one week. These bands are made of aluminum, have identification marks stamped on and cannot be removed because the bird's foot grows and prevents the band from slipping off.

The leg band may be put on either the right or the left leg. Two toes may be pushed forward, two backward, the band is slipped up the leg and the toes pulled out from under it. Personally we prefer bunching three toes together, leaving the smallest one free. The toes of budgerigars are jointed so that one toe may be pushed either to the front or back. The band slips easily over three toes and then the smallest is pulled out to free it from the band. If the band should

Opposite: A beautiful baby Lutino budgie, only a few weeks old. Cinnamons, Opalines, Albinos, Lutinos and Slates follow what is known as a sex-linked manner of inheritance. The reason for the sex linkage of these characters is that the genes for the characters are situated on the same chromosome pair that controls the sex of the birds.

not move smoothly across the joint, a little water will help.

Usually two birds, sometimes three, from one nest can be banded at the same time, but because the birds are of such graded sizes, repeated checking is necessary. Occasionally a band which was put on too small a foot will be found lying in the nest box and must be replaced. That all band numbers must be carefully recorded cannot be emphasized too often.

The following classification has been drawn up by ornithologists:

1. *Fledgling*—A bird which has left the nest, is still wearing all of its nest feathers, and is dependent on its parents for food and care.

1. The baby budgie ready to be banded with a closed band. 2. to 5. Steps showing how to slip on the band, which will remain with the bird for life.

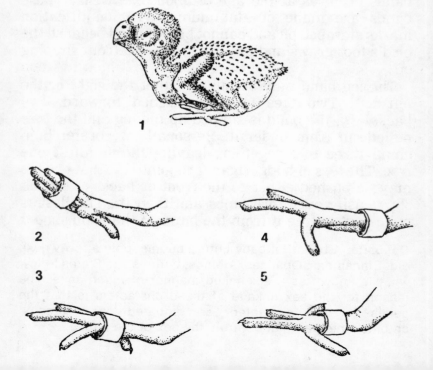

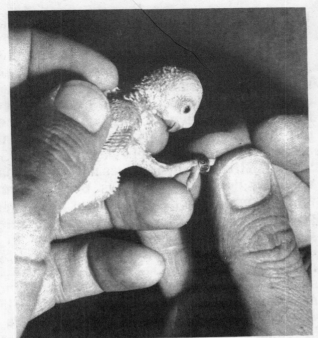

As the size of the feet of the individual chicks varies, it is necessary to watch the youngsters from the age of about five days onward so that their feet do not become too big for the bands to pass over.

2. *Juvenile*—A bird before its juvenile molt, but able to fend for itself and eat alone.

3. *Immature or Unflighted*—A bird which has completed its juvenile or baby molt, but still has its first growth of wing feathers.

4. *Young*—A bird under one year of age is called a young bird, even if it looks fully mature.

The Budgerigar Hen

The breeding hen deserves extra consideration. She plays the principal role in the propagation of her kind. She apparently carries the main responsibility in the breeding cage. Her maternal instincts are strong, so strong in fact that she has earned for herself the reputation of being vicious when in reality her outbreaks of temper are nine times out of ten prompted by a desire to defend her hearth or offspring. If she were as easy going as most cock budgerigars, there is no telling whether young would be raised at all.

In the wild state hens have to defend themselves, as well as small young which they are covering in the nest cavity. Perhaps this is the reason why their bite is so much stronger than that of the male. When an enemy approaches, the male, roosting outside, saves himself by flying away, even in the dark. All the hen can do is bite because the enemy, trying to enter through the nest hole, cuts off her only way of escape. She digs her beak into the enemy and does not let go, "hangs on like a bulldog," as the saying goes. Breeders, reaching into a nest box, have often pulled out a hen in this rather painful way.

The main reason for bloody fights in an aviary seems to be that two hens decide to occupy the same nest box. Therefore, breeders who use the colony system of breeding always supply about twice as many nest boxes as there are pairs of budgies. They are also extremely careful never to allow an extra hen in the breeding flight. An unmated hen can cause a great deal of trouble. Too long hours of artificial light will make birds nervous. A time clock set to turn on electric lights at daybreak and turn them off at sunset will eliminate nervousness caused by this source.

If any nutritional deficiencies exist, hens, as a rule, are affected more obviously than cocks. This is natural since the hen lays an enormous egg in proportion to her size. Most vices can be traced to a faulty diet. A calcium deficiency will cause soft-shelled eggs and the hen, as a consequence, may die egg-bound. Hens spend the major part of the breeding season in the dark nest box. If budgerigars are allowed to breed in the summer, this robs the hens of much sunshine. For these reasons the hens should be given special attention. If one of the outdoor flights is larger, or receives more sunshine, or is better constructed so as to allow rain to enter without causing damage, this flight should be chosen for the hens. At the same time it should be remembered that hens have a stronger desire to chew on woodwork than cocks. Therefore, pieces of soft wood, mortar, etc. should be kept about for the hens to satisfy their urge.

Most hens, if kept with only one cock in a breeding cage, will not easily take to another one. If, however, hens are kept in a flight by themselves when the breeding season is over, they will mate with a new cock the following season. A cock can be used with another hen during the same breeding season after a rest in the cock flight, providing he raised only one nest previously.

Some hens are not as bad tempered as their reputation makes them. At times, two have laid eggs, incubated them and raised their young in the same nest box. But such an occurrence is rare.

Cage Breeding versus Colony Breeding

The phases of budgerigar breeding under discussion in this book are, on the whole, applicable only to "controlled" breeding or breeding in cages, one pair to a cage. This is the best system by which a pedigree can be kept, a strain of line-bred birds built up and a high proportion of show specimens produced. The finer points of color breeding, such as crossing normal, well-known colors with rare shades can only be pursued if the exact parentage of each bird is known. Many cocks from such matings look normal but carry the blood of a rare color. Unless such a cock is mated in the proper way, the rare shade is kept from showing.

Colony breeding is the system of breeding a number of pairs in one large enclosure. When budgerigars were first bred in captivity this was the most widely used system, but gradually the disadvantages of colony breeding became apparent and "controlled" breeding—breeding single pairs in one enclosure or cage—has become more and more popular. The disadvantages of large enclosure uncontrolled breeding consist of a low yield of young per pair due to fighting, interference during the mating act, parent birds worn

Breeding in cages has quite a number of advantages over other methods. Single pairs can be housed in a cage, and the breeder is certain of the exact pedigree of all the youngsters produced.

out by raising too many young, overcrowded nests, too great a proportion of young with feather troubles, the appearance of too many green birds because all colors have been allowed to interbreed freely, etc. Although outdated, some colony breeding in large enclosures still exists in this country. Owners of some of these establishments are ignorant of the simplest rules by which budgerigars should be bred. In many cases they have never bothered to obtain information by reading current publications in the field. As an illustration—a public zoolgical garden allows its budgerigars to breed indiscriminately in one large enclosure. Young birds are left with the breeding flock and commence to breed while still immature. Old birds are allowed to raise nest after nest of young. As a result the flight becomes so crowded that it is necessary to eliminate some of the birds. About half of them, often the parents of helpless young in the nests, are trapped and removed. Sometimes the loud squealing of the orphans for food attracts other adult budgerigars and these give the helpless babies an occasional feeding, but this is more or less chance. Such breeding methods constitute not only cruelty to animals, but may endanger public health. Birds weakened by overbreeding are subject to diseases, some of which are communicable to other birds and to humans. Psittacosis in particular should be mentioned in this connection.

There are, of course, colony breeders who keep themselves informed of modern developments and have devised a system of more or less controlled breeding within the colony. They breed their birds in small compartments with only a few pairs to one enclosure. Young are removed as soon as they can fend for themselves and are not given breeding facilities until one year old. Adult breeding pairs are set up for breeding on the same date and breeding in such an enclosure is stopped after two nests have been raised. Third-clutch eggs are destroyed. Budgerigars are closed-banded, the bands carrying the year of birth, and records are kept. Birds of similar pedigree and color are kept in one enclosure.

It should be realized that no system of colony breeding offers any degree of certainty as to who is the father of a nest of young. Although hens in single breeding cages rarely take to another cock during the same season, they apparently often do get sufficiently acquainted with other cocks in the same breeding flight to produce young of such colors as could not have been fathered by their original mate. Even previous pairing up for about one week and then turning these pairs into a common enclosure does not guarantee that all young in a nest will have had the same father. Strict pedigree breeding, therefore, can hardly be carried

When budgies are housed in cages it is necessary that their diet be of a less fattening nature than that used for birds housed in an aviary. Breeders have found that three parts small canary seed, one part white millet and one part yellow millet makes a good standard feed. When chicks are in the nests a few whole or hulled oats can be added to the mixture. Another (but less preferred) mixture is one part Proso millet and one part canary seed. W. Watmough, the leading English authority on budgerigars, likes to give his birds two parts canary seed to one part millet, plus the following possible alternative additions: oats or groats, a quarter of the quantity of millet. Either of these can be a useful additive and help to reduce the cost of feeding. Provided the oats are of good quality they can be de-husked oats; the budgies will remove the husks from the oats, as they do with all husked seeds. Australian or Canadian wheat (not English, whose quality varies from year to year) is a good extra if provided in a small quantity, rather smaller than the proportion of oats.

out by any system of colony breeding. In most cases unrelated birds will have to be added at intervals and this may prove expensive.

Whether or not a breeder makes a success of breeding budgerigars by an improved, modern method of colony breeding depends on how much care he gives his birds and the amount of time he spends on keeping records. Color breeding with a certain guarantee of the color factors of the young can be carried out if the breeder takes the trouble to study underlying principles. If all hens in one enclosure are, for instance, Cinnamon hens and all cocks are normal, then an up-to-date breeder knows that all young cocks produced will be split cinnamon cocks and all young hens normal hens. Such systems can be worked out by studying the genetics of the budgerigar.

Feeding

The usual seed mixture is one part Proso millet and one part canary seed. One-half teaspoon of plain cod-liver oil is added to each pound of seeds and mixed well. Some breeders prefer using more canary seeds than millet. Oats are fed in separate containers, more in cold weather, and to parents feeding young and to growing young in the flight. Unhulled oats are best. Less or no oats are fed to resting adult birds and in warm weather. A moderate amount of greens should be fed daily. Fresh water must be supplied. A good grit consists of half ground oystershell and half granite, ocean, or brown gravel. A piece of cuttlefish bone should be hung up in each cage. When parents are feeding young, a good nestling food of high protein content should be given daily.

Many diseases and breeding troubles are caused by a poor state of nutrition. We therefore strongly advise breeders to acquaint themselves with the principles underlying good nutrition as outlined in the book "Modern Feeding of Budgerigars."* Faulty feather growth is often caused by inadequate feeding and has been fully discussed in the book "Diseases of Budgerigars."* There is joy and happiness in store for the fancier when he can watch a group of healthy, lively budgerigars in their shiny coat of feathers.

* Published by T.F.H. Publications Inc., Neptune, N.J.

II. Genetics

Chromosomes and Genes

The science of genetics is the study of heredity. We believe that breeders, in order to produce the best birds, should have some knowledge of the influence of heredity on breeding. We shall, therefore, outline a few fundamentals which may interest the practical breeder.

A living organism, be it animal, plant, or bird, is made up of cells. Each cell has a nucleus which consists largely of chromatin. When an organism is growing its cells divide. The chromatin of the nucleus breaks up into chromosomes which are arranged in pairs; each of these splits lengthwise, one half going to one daughter cell, the other half going to the other daughter cell.

Each species has its own set number of chromosomes, varying greatly in number in different kinds of animals and plants. The human body has forty-six chromosomes in each cell, or twenty-three pairs. A budgerigar has fifty-eight, or twenty-nine pairs. In the germ cells (the reproductive cells), however, only half the number of chromosomes are present due to a previous reduction division. The sperm carries the reproductive chromosomes of the male; the egg or ovum that of the female. When the sperm penetrates the egg, the combination of both sets of chromosomes brings the number up to that contained in the other body cells of the species—for instance, forty-six chromosomes in the human, fifty-eight in the budgerigar.

Most bird breeders have heard of "genes" carrying hereditary factors. They have been defined as units of inheritance and can be pictured as minute disks arranged like a string of beads and constituting the body of the chromosome. A chromosome, therefore, consists of innumerable tiny, flat units called genes. Most genes act in groups.

Before genes became known, hereditary factors were believed to be carried in the blood. "Blooded" animals are those which have been purebred for generations. The terms "bloodlines" and "adding new blood" are still being used because everyone knows what they mean.

The normal varieties of budgerigars inherit color in accordance with the Mendelian laws of inheritance. These laws were carefully worked out for budgerigars in many breeding tests by the German geneticist Dr. Hans Duncker, with the help of Cunsul Cremer. The

LEFT: Representation of a body cell. **a.** cell nucleus. **b. cell wall. c.** one of the many pairs of chromosomes. **d.** the X chromosome. **e.** the Y chromosome, which probably does not carry any genes. RIGHT: Representation of a pair of chromosomes on a large scale, showing the genes as small discs. (In reality there are many more genes in a chromosome.)

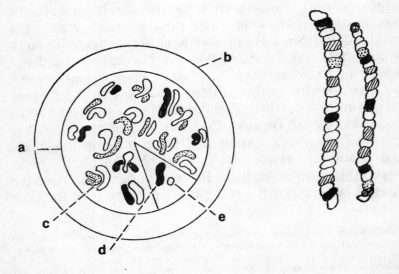

fundamental example is the mating of Green to Blue which gives us one hundred percent Green/blue young.* These young mated with each other give us twenty-five percent Green, fifty percent Green/blue (Green split blue) and twenty-five percent Blue. Green is dominant, Blue is recessive. The inheritance of rare colors, however, is much more complicated and in many instances cannot be expressed in percentages since too many alterations in the genes enter in.

Mutation

Changes in the genes bring about what is called mutation. When suddenly in a strain of purebred animals or plants an individual is produced which radically differs in appearance or constitution from its brothers and sisters, and when this individual passes its new character on to its offspring, a mutation has taken place. The parents have thrown a sport. Mutations in animals and plants have been brought about in scientific laboratories by irradiation with X-rays and neutrons; this, however, often causes sterility. Also alcohol treatment, hormone treatment, serum therapy, and changes in temperature have brought about mutations. One cage bird breeder washed a clutch of eggs in warm water to remove dirt. All young which hatched were albinos. As the breeder did not know the exact state of incubation when the eggs were washed, nor the temperature of the water used, he was never able to produce the same effect again. This was recorded by the Duke of Bedford. As yet not enough is known to warrant experimentation on cage birds by the practical breeder. It is advisable in our cage to leave things up to nature. But the budgerigar breeder should be constantly on the alert for any new form or

---

*A split is indicated by the slanted dividing line: green/blue (= green split blue) and indicates that, though the bird is a visual green, it carries a recessive (hidden factor) for blue and if bred to a bird of the recessive color series, will produce a percentage of the recessive color progeny which will be pure for that color. A budgie can only be split to a recessive character, never to a dominant.

color which may appear among his birds. Mutations are less rare than hitherto supposed. Budgerigars have produced more sports than any other cage birds.

We hear much about "split" budgerigars. We know chromosomes appear in pairs. If a group of genes on one chromosome has mutated and not on the other, this mutation may not show. The bird is split to the new color—the new color in this instance is recessive, which means it is hidden. Only inbreeding or line breeding will bring it out. If the mutation has been a dominant one then its first appearance will not be hidden but visible.

If a mutation has taken place in a sex chromosome the new character will be a sex-linked one. We may suspect a sex-linked mutation if the birds first showing it are all hens.

X and Y Chromosomes

The two members of each pair of chromosomes are similar in size and shape. However, there is one pair of sex chromosomes among the others. In male birds the two members of this pair are similar and are both called X chromosomes. In female birds one member of the pair is much smaller and is called the Y chromosome. The normal sized member of the pair is called the X chromosome. A male bird has two X chromosomes, a female bird has one X and one Y chromosome. A sex-linked character is carried only on the female's X chromosome, but on both chromosomes of the male. Therefore, if a female belongs to a sex-linked variety she cannot be split. She either shows the color of the sex-linked variety or she does not. If she does not show it, she is normal and carries no blood of the sex-linked variety. A male bird, however, may look normal but may be split to a sex-linked variety.

Sex-Linkage

Characters passed on from parents to offspring by

the genes in other than the sex chromosomes will be inherited by the young males and females alike. They are "normal" birds which means they are not sex-linked. "Normal" budgerigars are those which belong to our normally colored varieties, such as the well-known Greens, Blues, Yellows, and White Blues. A normal Green split blue (Green/blue) crossed with a normal Blue will throw half Green/blue and half Blue young. There is no sex-linkage, consequently either cocks or hens may be green or blue.

Characters passed on by the genes in the sex chromosomes will show a sex-linkage. Such birds when bred to normal colors will, in certain matings, produce young cocks of one color and young hens of another color. Or the young cocks will look normal but be split to the sex-linked variety. The young hens, if normal looking, will not be split to a sex-linked variety but may be split to another color or an N.S.L. variety. It helps to remember that when normal hens are in the nest of one normal and one sex-linked parent, these hens never carry any blood of the sex-linked variety. The young cocks from such a mating are split to the sex-linked variety because cocks have two large X chromosomes. One of these may carry the genes of the sex-linked variety, the other of the normal variety. The Y chromosome of the hen is small and probably does not carry any genes. The following table gives theoretical expectations. Cinnamons have been taken as an example.

Summarizing the expectations of young from Cinnamon and normal birds, we obtain:

1. Cinnamon cock to Cinnamon hen = both cocks and hens Cinnamon.
2. Cinnamon cock to normal hen = split Cinnamon cocks and Cinnamon hens.
3. Split Cinnamon cock to Cinnamon hen = Cinnamon cocks, Cinnamon hens, split Cinnamon cocks, and normal hens.
4. Split Cinnamon cock to normal hen = normal cocks,

split Cinnamon cocks, normal hens and Cinnamon hens.
5. Normal cock to Cinnamon hen = split Cinnamon cocks and normal hens.

When crossing Cinnamons with normal colors, it should be remembered that normal colors are dominant over Cinnamons, even such light shades as yellow and white. The Cinnamon factor is recessive and will not show in the male if only one gene is carrying it. In the female the Cinnamon factor cannot be recessive. It either is present and shows, or it is not present and the bird is normal. A Cinnamon Green hen may be split to blue, yellow, and white.

The symbol used for the sex-linked inheritance of budgerigars is S.L. The normal colors, which do not carry their color genes in the sex chromosomes, have a non-sex-linked inheritance (N.S.L.). In addition to the Cinnamon, the Albino, Lutino, and Opaline varieties are also sex-linked. However, N.S.L. varieties of Albinos and Lutinos have been bred. The expectations in the above table will be found to be true in the majority of cases. It has happened, however, that actual breeding results occasionally differ. This may be due to the fact that different mutations are involved though the birds outwardly appear to be the same. Crossing with Yellow Faces, for example, has brought about some surprising results. Budgerigars that follow the pattern of S.L. include Albino, Cinnamon, Lutino and Opaline.

Sex Ratio

An enormous amount of writing has been done on ways and means to influence sex ratio. Quack medicines, "money back guarantees," etc., have deceived many people. When eggs are fertilized by the sperm of the cock, about an equal number of cocks and hens should develop in the eggs. However, this ratio is often disturbed by several factors. Some chicks die in the shell. If these are of one sex, more of the other sex will hatch. Then, too, some young chicks die in the nest soon after hatching. If these belong to one sex, more birds of the opposite sex will grow up.

Some aviaries constantly produce more cocks, others, more hens. It seems that conditions under which these birds are raised tend to suppress one sex or the other. There may be certain factors which have a harmful effect on cocks only. In such an aviary more hens will be produced. In other aviaries, where more cocks hatch and grow up, some factors seem to be at work which cause females to die in the shell or when very young. There are families of birds in the same aviary, kept under identical conditions, which consistently produce more hens, others more cocks.

The predominance of one sex over the other is often due to inheritance. Other factors too may be responsible. A radical change in diet may bring about a different sex ratio. Environmental conditions play a role. It also has been observed that large nests have a different sex ratio than small nests. This means that small nests result from the death of only one sex during early stages of growth.

Some breeders have observed a different sex ratio during different seasons of the year, for instance, more hens at the beginning of the breeding season and more cocks at the end. Also, it has been claimed that hens which are induced to breed before reaching good all-around breeding condition produce more cocks than hens. Old hens mated to young cocks are supposed to produce more males. These statements have not been proved. Sex ratio is influenced by so many factors, some still unknown, that it will take an enormous amount of carefully controlled experiments before we know precisely what these influences are.

An aviary which produces each year an almost equal number of cocks and hens, with few dead in shell or dying at an early age, probably had conditions close to the ideal. Too often, each year brings various troubles, some affecting sex ratio, some not. When sex ratio is affected in a way not desired by the breeder, it is a good plan to alter temperature, food or general management. One of these conditions may be responsible for the suppression of one sex or the other.

Breeders of canaries have sometimes noticed abnormal sex ratios when crossing canaries with finches, like siskins, etc. As a rule the cocks are the ones which survive, while the hens succumb either in the egg or shortly after hatching.

On top of the nest box sits a Lutino cock which is not of show quality but produces good pet birds. The hen below is an Opaline Skyblue hen, a popular color that is almost always available in pet stores.

Inheritance and Environment

How much modification of traits is due to inheritance and how much to environment has been a subject of discussion ever since man knew that certain characters are passed on from parents to offspring. Research on hereditary traits, for that reason, has to be controlled very carefully. All outward influences have to be exactly the same before any studies on heredity can be undertaken. Also the subjects have to be chosen with special regard to their physical makeup. They should be as alike as possible or results will be misleading. Therefore, geneticists working on hereditary traits of laboratory animals use in-bred stock and guard against any deficiencies in their food.

The subject of the relationship of heredity to disease is a complex one. Enough work has been done, however, to state definitely that there is such a relationship. Strains of laboratory animals have been produced which are immune to certain diseases, while other strains are susceptible. Tumor formation has been found to be of a hereditary nature in some cases. Dead embryos in the shell or death of young in the nest may be caused by heredity. Sterility may be hereditary. This sounds like a paradox, because if there are no offspring how can anything be inherited? The answer is that many hereditary factors are passed on in the split or heterozygous form. Thus a bird may carry a recessive which, if combined with another recessive factor of the same kind, will produce lethal genes which kill the embryo. These will cause "dead in shell."

The susceptibility of certain strains of birds to virus and bacterial diseases is now clearly recognized. Faulty feather growth (like French Molt in budgerigars), malformation of beaks, etc., have been produced in the hereditary form. Bad traits, unfortunately, can be transmitted as well as good ones.

Size of eggs, type, color, size of birds, and many other factors are inherited. Well-informed poultry men do not buy stock of unknown origin and mix it with their own.

Large commercial poultry farms of so-called barnyard fowl without pedigree do not pay attention to possible hereditary traits and freely add to their stock from any source. Such flocks have demonstrated that they are far less profitable than inbred stock of known heredity. These findings are beginning to be recognized by cage bird breeders, who now pay more and more attention to heredity and careful selection.

Favorable environmental conditions tend to suppress undesirable hereditary traits in some instances. On the other hand, birds not afflicted with bad heredity may develop malformations, poor feather growth, infertility, susceptibility to diseases, and other troubles if kept under conditions impairing their health. Improper care and feeding, bad housing, high temperature, daylight periods which are too long or too short, lack of cleanliness, and similar conditions will cause disease and breeding troubles in the best strains.

Certain vitamin deficiencies have caused the same manifestations of disease in the acute form as have been observed in strains which carried such troubles in the hereditary form. Research dealing with these problems is constantly under way in scientific laboratories. Any worker in this field recognizes the immense complexity of the inter-relation between hereditary and environmental influences. If we try to keep both at their best in our aviary, we can avoid much disappointment and loss.

Building a Strain

The goal of an ambitious breeder is to develop his own strain which conforms to the ideal of his breed, but still shows certain characters found only in birds from his aviary. Such a breeder, wherever his birds may be, will recognize them from many others. Patience and persistence in the face of disappointments are necessary. The breeder must strive constantly to translate the picture in his mind into reality.

There is a saying, "A good breeder is born, not made." This is probably true. A combination of certain inborn

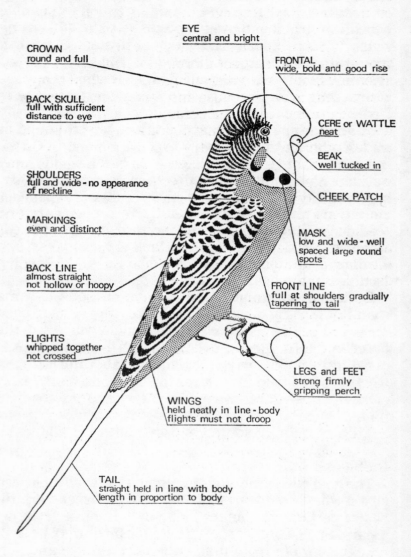

EYE
central and bright

CROWN
round and full

FRONTAL
wide, bold and good rise

BACK SKULL
full with sufficient
distance to eye

CERE or WATTLE
neat

BEAK
well tucked in

SHOULDERS
full and wide - no appearance
of neckline

CHEEK PATCH

MARKINGS
even and distinct

MASK
low and wide - well
spaced large round
spots

BACK LINE
almost straight
not hollow or hoopy

FRONT LINE
full at shoulders gradually
tapering to tail

FLIGHTS
whipped together
not crossed

LEGS and FEET
strong firmly
gripping perch.

WINGS
held neatly in line - body
flights must not droop

TAIL
straight held in line with body
length in proportion to body

The main features of a budgerigar. Drawing reproduced by
permission of the Budgerigar Society.

characteristics of a person tend to make him successful or unsuccessful. However, nothing can be achieved without effort. The breeder should know first what he wants. If it is to build his own strain of first class birds, he should study the subject thoroughly. He should be conscientious, not easily discouraged, and when things go wrong, search for the cause and remedy it. If his efforts have been crowned with success, he should recognize his good fortune and safeguard it as best he can. He should not become negligent and try to coast along on what he has accomplished. Most success is based on steady hard work, not intermittent spurts of enthusiasm. Faithful, long range devotion to this hobby will pay dividends in more ways than one.

On the opposite page is the illustration issued to all members of the Budgerigar Society (England) and below the current Budgerigar Society Ideal Budgerigar Standard, plus the Society 'Scale of points' which emphasizes those features regarded as significant for judging.

CONDITION is essential. If a bird is not in condition it should never be considered for any award.

TYPE—Gracefully tapered from nape of neck to tip of tail, with an approximately straight back line, and a rather deep nicely curved chest.

LENGTH—The ideal length is 8½ in. from the crown of the head to the tip of the tail. Wings well braced, carried just above the cushion of the tail and not crossed. The ideal length of the wing is 3¾ in. from the butt to the tip of the longest primary flight, which must contain seven visual primary flight feathers fully grown and not broken. *No bird showing 'long-flighted' characteristics shall be eligible to take any award.*

HEAD—Large, round, wide and symmetrical when viewed from any angle; curvature of skull commencing at cere, to lift outward and upward, continuing over the top and to base of head in one graceful sweep.

BEAK—Set well into face.

EYE—To be bold and bright, and positioned well away from front, top and back skull.

NECK—To be short and wide when viewed from either side or front.

WINGS—Approximately two-fifths the total length of the bird, well braced, carried just above the cushion of the tail and not crossed.

TAIL—To be straight and tight with two long tail feathers.

POSITION—Steady on perch at an angle of 30 degrees from the vertical, looking fearless and natural.

MASK AND SPOTS—Mask to be clear, deep and wide, and where demanded by the Standard should be ornamented by six evenly spaced large round throat spots, the outer two being partially covered at the base by cheek patches, the size of the spots to be in proportion to the rest of the make-up of the bird as shown in the illustrated Ideal. Spots can be either too large or too small.

LEGS AND FEET—Legs should be straight and strong, and two front and two rear toes and claws firmly gripping perch.

MARKINGS—Wavy markings on cheek, head, neck, back and wings to stand out clearly.

COLOUR—Clear and level and of an even shade.

save for charts

The Budgerigar Society's Scale of Points

REVISED SCALE OF POINTS Remember: Condition is Supremely Important	Size shape balance and deportment	Size and shape of head	Colour	Mask and spots	Wing markings
Green (Light, Dark or Olive)	45	20	15	15	5
Grey Green (Light, Medium or Dark) ..	45	20	15	15	5
Yellow (incldg. Op. Yell. but excldg. Lutino)	45	20	35	—	—
Olive Yellow (including Cinnamon Olive Yellow)	45	20	35	—	—
Skyblue, Cobalt, Mauve or Violet ..	45	20	15	15	5
Grey (Light, Medium or Dark)	45	20	15	15	5
White (Light Suffusion including Opaline White but excluding Albino)	45	20	*35	—	—
Whitewing (Skyblue, Cobalt, Mauve, Violet or Grey)	45	20	*35	—	—
Yellow-wing (Light, Dark, Olive or Grey Green)	45	20	*35	—	—

This photo of a budgie shows a much-admired color phase. The bird is a Normal Violet and is of good size and substance, particularly for this beautiful color phase.

REVISED SCALE OF POINTS Remember: Condition is Supremely Important	Size shape balance and deportment	Size and shape of head	Colour	Mask and spots	Wing markings
Greywing (Light, Dark, Olive or Grey Green)	45	20	10	10	15
Greywing (Skyblue, Cobalt, Mauve, Violet or Grey)	45	20	10	10	15
Cinnamon (Light, Dark, Olive or Grey Green)	45	20	10	10	15
Cinnamon (Skyblue, Cobalt, Mauve, Violet or Grey)	45	20	10	10	15
Fallow (Light, Dark, Olive or Grey Green)	45	20	15	15	5
Fallow (Skyblue, Cobalt, Mauve, Violet or Grey)	45	20	15	15	5
Lutino	45	20	35	—	—
Albino	45	20	35	—	—
Opaline (Light, Dark, Olive or Grey Green)	40	20	†25	10	5
Opaline (Skyblue, Cobalt, Mauve, Violet or Grey)	40	20	†25	10	5
Opaline Cinnamon (Light, Dark, Olive or Grey Green)	40	20	†25	10	5
Opaline Cinnamon (Skyblue, Cobalt, Mauve, Violet or Grey)	40	20	†25	10	5
Opaline Greywing (Light, Dark, Olive or Grey Green)	40	20	†25	10	5
Opaline Greywing (Skyblue, Cobalt, Mauve, Violet or Grey)	40	20	†25	10	5
Yellow-faced (All varieties in Blue series except Pieds)	45	20	15	15	5
Pied (Dominant varieties)	45	20	§15	10	‡10
Pied (Clear Flighted varieties)	45	20	10	10	¶15
Pied (Recessive varieties)..	45	20	‡20	—	‡15
Dark-eyed Clear varieties	45	20	35	—	—
Lacewings	45	20	10	10	15

* Points allocated for depth of colour and clearness of wings.

† Including clear mantle and neck (10 points).

‡ Including contrast in variegation.

¶ Including clear flights and tail.

§ Includes band.

Teams of six birds of any one colour or teams of four birds of any one colour. Points: General quality, 50; Uniformity, 50.

Foundation Stock

The beginner should not hesitate long about what stock to purchase when starting to breed cage birds. The best will prove the cheapest in the end. If he buys pedigreed, line-bred foundation stock, he will save many years of work. First class birds do not eat any more or require any more care than cheap stock. Yet they bring higher prices when properly bred and cared for. All livestock varies in price according to its quality and breeding. Line-bred canaries and budgerigars of exhibition quality are necessarily priced much higher than ordinary birds of the same species; they are worth more. They also have a longer life expectancy because they have been bred with great care (not been overbred) and have been fed the best foods, and they are less subject to disease than are birds of poor stock. Quality counts—and must be paid for.

Mating Procedures

We are concerned here only with the breeding of pedigree stock, not with uncontrolled colony breeding. Single pairs are kept in separate breeding compartments, each of these is numbered and hen and cock recorded by their closed leg band numbers. Sire and dam of each young leaving the nest are known. Each young has been closed banded when only a few days old and there is no doubt of its pedigree. The possibility of any chance mating has been excluded.

The following are different systems of building a strain. Any one may be used, but all overlap in certain respects. They are: (1) Selection, (2) Inbreeding, (3) Prepotency, (4) Line breeding, and (5) Outcrossing. In discussing these systems we shall again have to talk about genes, the bearers of heredity. Genes are arranged in pairs. If one gene of the pair responsible for a certain character is different from the corresponding one in the other chromosome, the bird is called

It was John Gould who brought the first living budgerigar to Europe in 1840. From then on these hardy little birds were imported in increasing numbers. As Hans Steiner, in a study published in Zurich, Switzerland, pointed out, there developed during this period a steadily growing interest in keeping birds and other animals in captivity. Zoological gardens were founded and books on ornithology and aviculture were published. At the end of the 19th century, 600,000 pairs of living budgerigars were imported to England, and breeders in the Netherlands soon distinguished themselves by raising these birds. The first large aviary for this purpose was built in the Zoological Garden of Antwerp around 1870, although small establishments had already been in existence since 1850.

Fabulous prices were paid for new colors as long as they were still scarce. A Japanese prince, in 1925, was so intrigued by the beautiful blue color (right) he saw in England that he purchased one pair and took it home to Japan to give it to his bride-to-be as a love-token. From then on a vogue developed in Japan to give a pair of blue lovebirds (budgerigars) to one's loved ones, and prices went up to a thousand dollars. A short time later, however, prices fell again. The Japanese, being experienced in raising all kinds of birds, started to raise blue budgies themselves; furthermore the importation of these birds was stopped by the Japanese government. Thus ended the most prosperous period for English breeders, but the name "lovebird" still clings to the little budgerigar.

heterozygous for this character. He is not purebred, but split; or, we may say, he is not double factor, but single factor. If both genes of the pair are the same, the bird is homozygous for this trait; he shows the trait in his outward appearance; he is double factor. If a bird is heterozygous, one gene will be dominant, the other recessive. The former is visible, the latter hidden. By certain methods of mating the latter will show itself. The character then has changed from heterozygous to homozygous. To achieve this, to bring out hidden characters, a strain is subjected to inbreeding.

1. **Selection.** This method of mating is widely used by cage bird breeders and is often, not quite correctly, called line breeding. From the flock of breeding birds certain individuals are selected which, in their outward appearance, come close to what the breeder desires to show in his birds. Their offspring are kept for further propagation. The young of unselected birds are disposed of. Undesirable features will show in some birds and these will be culled (removed from the flocks because inferior). Culling promotes uniformity in the strain. However, culling will have to be continued indefinitely and will mean a loss.

Success in making a wise selection of which birds to keep and which to cull largely depends on the good judgment of the breeder. If he has his mind fixed on one character, he may develop a blind spot for some other equally important points. He should know which characters are most important and which are less so. If he selects for too many qualities, the selection will of necessity be weak. What he has to learn is to select for a number of important characters and cull on that line. Some minor good characters may have to be sacrificed in order to bring out major points. If too little attention is paid to culling, the work of years will be lost or the strain will never develop into an outstanding one.

Taking into account the merits of relatives of a bird

under consideration may help the breeder decide whether to keep or cull a bird. Relatives consist of two groups, those from which the bird descended and those which he produced. Studying the former is called the pedigree test, studying the latter the progeny test.

If the system of selection is adopted by a breeder, he must continue to select for the same characteristics, or other features will soon creep out in his strain. The reason for this is that all genes have not been made homozygous by inbreeding; many remain heterozygous. The birds remain split to other features. These, however, will not show when selection on the same line is kept up. Some of these heterozygous or split features may never manifest themselves in the homozygous form; therefore, selection is not as good a method to establish characters as is inbreeding.

A popular mating method used by cage bird breeders is to select the best birds and mate them, then select the second best and mate them, and so on down the line. This method alone does not reduce variability in a strain. The best pair may produce young not as good as the second or third best pair. Good points remain scattered unless a system of inbreeding is adopted at the same time. However, selection is a better method than random mating and is recommended for the beginner who has not yet found his favorite mating procedure.

Sometimes genes of a mediocre pair of birds combine in such a way that superior young are produced. Such a pair "nicks." The value of the superior young again depends on the strain. If much previous selection was done intelligently, or if the strain was inbred or linebred, the young of the pair which "nicks" will be of higher value than otherwise.

2. Inbreeding. The mating of close relatives is called inbreeding. There is some likeness among relatives but they are not always as closely related as one might think. For instance, two brothers of unrelated stock

Left: Pied Mauve. *Center:* Dominant Dutch Pied Olive Green.
Right: Australian Dominant Pied Opaline Gray Green.

Left: Recessive Yellow Face Blue. *Center:* Recessive Pied
Skyblue. *Right:* Australian Pied Whiteflight.

Left: Australian Banded Pied Yellowface Cobalt. *Center:* Australian Banded Pied Opaline Olive Green. *Right:* Australian Pied Opaline Blue.

Left: Australian Pied Normal Cobalt. *Center:* Australian Pied Normal Dark Green. *Right:* Australian Pied Opaline Skyblue.

are fifty percent related, not one hundred percent. If we purchase the brother of a prize winner, only half of his genes will be the same as those of the prize bird.

If both parents of a bird are related to each other more or less closely, the two brothers will look more similar. Mathematical formulas could be applied to show the percentage of relationships of two brothers when bred from related stock. When we purchase a bird from a prize winning family, we like to know how good our chance is to produce prize winners from this bird. This depends entirely on how much inbreeding or line breeding has been done in this strain of birds. To fix characters, inbreeding is a necessity.

We shall first examine the merits of inbreeding and later take up some of the difficulties that may be encountered while following this line of mating procedure. All famous breeds of livestock have been created by inbreeding.

The great advantage of inbreeding is in fixing characters and reducing variation. Birds bred from an inbred strain for certain show characters, color, or voice will breed young with these characters predominant. There will always be a few young which have to be culled because even the best inbred strains cannot be entirely perfect. If we breed birds from random matings, not related, we do not know what we will get. Even if these birds look fine on the outside, their young will show tremendous variation. If we want good birds, we must do a great deal of culling at first. While breeding unrelated stock from various sources, we may find a good specimen here and there. Such birds are called "flash in the pan." Their genes are not fixed in definite combinations. When bred, the good points of such birds will be dispersed again and we will obtain mediocre young. For this reason some prize winners have proved a great disappointment in the breeding room. Pedigree is worth more than looks.

No inbred and highly pedigreed strain will be perfect. There are too many chromosomes, too many

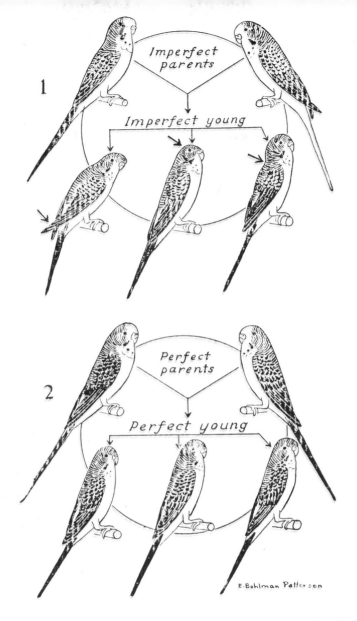

1. Imperfections illustrated in young are faults in (left to right): posture, head, wing carriage.

2. Line-bred stock of very good type. All young budgies show striations over forehead and indefinite throat spots.

Left: Fallow Light Green. *Center:* Fallow Cobalt. *Right:* Crested Normal Cobalt (with neck mane).

Left: Dark-eyed Clear White. *Center:* Lutino. *Right:* Tufted Normal Dark Green.

Left: Half Circular Crested Normal Cobalt. *Center:* Halfsider Recessive Pied Cobalt. *Right:* Dutch Pied Clearflight Light Green.

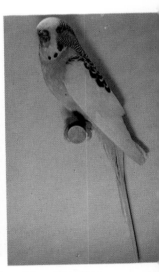

Left: Tufted Normal Skyblue. *Center:* Quartersider Opaline Dark Green-Cobalt. *Right:* Australian Banded Pied Normal Green.

genes and other factors influencing the appearance of the birds. Therefore, the breeding of cage birds remains a sport and a challenge to our gambling spirit. Surprises never cease and a sense of adventure spurs us on even if bad luck in the breeding room has put a temporary damper on our enthusiasm. By breeding good birds instead of indifferent ones, we may produce a great champion.

There is no set rule covering the method of building a reliable strain. Matings of son to granddam and daughter to grandsire are, as a rule, preferred to brother and sister matings. Most breeders avoid frequent brother and sister matings, because this most intense method of inbreeding tends to bring out too many undesirable characters at once and too much culling becomes necessary. Continued brother and sister matings may be used more extensively among mammals than among small cage birds. What relatives are to be used will depend on the quality of the foundation stock.

The novice who has acquired good birds would be wise to adopt a moderate inbreeding program. The better the birds the closer they may be inbred without much culling. Half-brother to sister, cousins or grandsire to granddaughter are used now and then, second cousins frequently. In this way a strain will be kept vigorous, and good points will be fixed.

This type of breeding should not be used with nondescript, unrelated stock unless the breeder wants to discard a great number of birds. Aviaries with no set breeding schedule, practicing uncontrolled breeding without pedigree, rarely use related birds. They advertise their stock as unrelated and, in order to keep it so, must constantly add new birds. If this is neglected and some inbreeding occurs, signs of degeneration will soon be noticed in many birds.

Opposite: This Gray hen was big, bold, steady in the showcage and a grand worker in the nesting season. She is pictured here at an advanced age. The novice would be wise to adopt better birds to produce great champions.

Left: Graywing Olive Green. *Center:* Normal Yellow. *Right:* Olive Green.

Left: Graywing Cobalt. *Center:* Yellow Face Graywing Skyblue. *Right:* Normal Graywing Skyblue.

Left: Yellow Wing Light Green. *Center:* Yellow Wing Dark Green. *Right:* Normal Cinnamon Graygreen.

Left: Whitewing Skyblue. *Center:* Whitewing Cobalt. *Right:* Normal Cinnamon Violet.

This brings us to the disadvantages of inbreeding. Birds of poor stock, when inbred, show up so badly that many people shy away from any inbred stock. They point to the poor cripples produced by mating relatives as proof of the disastrous effects of inbreeding. They also point to the occasional poor specimen found among a good strain of inbred birds and blame this on inbreeding. They forget that poor specimens frequently appear among unrelated birds or that other circumstances may affect the quality of birds. Some bad features are not inherited but are the result of poor housing, too long hours under artificial light after sundown, poor feeding, overbreeding, lack of wing exercises, etc. Birds suffering from vitamin deficiencies do not make good material for inbreeding. For all these reasons inbreeding has a bad reputation and bird breeders try to avoid the term.

3. **Prepotency.** If we have an outstanding cock and notice that this bird passes his characteristics on to his offspring in a plainly visible manner and that his young resemble each other and their sire to an unusual degree, then this cock possesses prepotency. Offspring are bred back to the outstanding sire, which brings us to line breeding.

4. **Line Breeding.** This method of breeding is widely used and popular among cage bird breeders. It is inbreeding in a modified sense. Line breeding is the system of breeding offspring back to one outstanding ancestor. If a pedigree is drawn up and the sire is connected with each of his offspring of a strain line-bred to one cock, each line of descent will lead to this cock. The dams will also be related to this cock. Finally all birds from this strain will be more or less closely related to each other and all will be related to the chosen cock. As long as that cock is alive and fertile, pedigree lines will go back directly to him. Later matings will proceed in a way to safeguard as close a relation as possible to this one cock and his descendants. The chosen bird may, of course, be a hen.

Line breeding means breeding related birds, but they are not, as a rule, as closely related as in inbreeding. Success in line breeding depends on the skill of the breeder in selecting the outstanding bird whose likeness he wants to impress on the birds in his aviary. This bird should possess a high degree of homozygosity. He should not be a "flash in the pan."

The breeder, in trying to find the best bird for the purpose of line breeding to it, should avail himself of all methods to determine its value. He should examine pedigrees, make progeny tests, and examine the bird's record on the show bench.

5. Outcrossing. A time may come when a strain, inbred or linebred for many generations, may show signs of weakening. Size begins to decrease, fertility is not as high as desired, and general stamina seems to suffer. If this should happen, the breeder first must check up on other causes, such as inferior seeds, infection, mites, etc. If he is convinced that the trouble lies in genetic weakness, he will decide on an outcross. He obtains a bird from a fellow breeder to bring "fresh blood" into his strain.

A bird chosen to be introduced into an inbred or linebred stud must come up to certain requirements. He or she must have been bred on similar lines to avoid introducing undesirable genes into the highly inbred and perfected strain. The addition of a bird with many inferior heterozygous or hidden characters will ruin the work of years. The breeder looking for a bird to be used as an outcross in his strain must try to obtain one from the related stud of another breeder. It may be argued that a related bird would not bring in fresh blood. We do not want too much fresh blood, or our efforts at building a strain would be ruined.

6. Test Matings. It is sometimes difficult to tell a purebred budgie from a split one. Among the Greens we have the pure Greens, the Green/yellows, the Green/blues and the Green/whites. In most cases the pure can be differentiated from the split Greens only

Left: Opaline Cinnamon Skyblue. *Center:* Opaline Cobalt. *Right:* Skyblue.

Left: Normal Mauve. *Center:* Normal Gray. *Right:* Normal Violet.

Left: Yellow Face Opaline Mauve. *Center:* Opaline Gray Green. *Right:* Opaline Olive Green.

Left: Normal Light Green. *Center:* Normal Dark Green Cock. *Right:* Yellow Face Skyblue.

by test matings when adult. There are, however, some experienced breeders who can tell the different breeds apart by turning the young birds on their backs while still in their baby feathers and examining the feather color on the under side, especially toward the vent. The color will be deeper in the pure birds. It will bear a distinct bluish tinge in the Green/blues and this will be considerably lighter in the Green/whites. The same holds true for the pure and split Blues and Yellows. Splits always show a fainter color toward the vent. There will always be some birds which evade correct classification. The shade of these seems to be that of an intermediate color. These birds must be mated later in such a way that by their offspring the breeder can figure out to which group the parent belonged.

Suppose we have a Sky Blue hen and want to find out whether she is pure or split white. She should be mated to a white cock. If she is pure, all young will be Blue/white (Blue split white); they will all look blue. If she is split white, half of the young will be white.

Sky Blue/white x White Sky Blue =
50% Sky Blue/white
50% White Sky Blue

Green/blue x Sky Blue =
50% Green/blue
50% Sky Blue

If the green bird is not split blue but pure, all young will look green but all are split blue. If two full colored budgerigars are mated and an occasional White is found in the nests, then both parents are split white.

If we want to test a green bird for being split to yellow, we mate him to a Yellow. If we obtain yellow young among the green, we know he actually is split yellow. The same rules apply to other splits. This applies to the normal, not the sex-linked varieties.

III Color Breeding

Before discussing the principal colors of budgerigars, we like to acquaint the reader with the color standard as published by The Budgerigar Society (England). It represents a valuable guide and should be studied by judges, exhibitors, breeders, and dealers. We have changed the spelling to that used in America.

The Standard

LIGHT GREEN
Mask: buttercup yellow, ornamented by six evenly spaced large round black throat spots, the outer two being partially covered at the base by cheek patches. Cheek patches: violet. General body color: back, rump, breast, flanks and underparts bright grass green of a solid and even shade throughout. Markings: on cheeks, back of head, neck and wings, black and well defined on a buttercup ground. Tail: long feathers, bluish black.

DARK GREEN
As above but with a dark laurel green body color. Tail: long feathers, darker in proportion.

OLIVE GREEN
As above but with a deep olive green body color. Tail: long feathers, darker in proportion.

GRAY GREEN
The Gray Green conforms to the standard for Light Green except in the following details. Cheek patches: gray to slate. General body color: dull mustard green. Tail: long feathers, black. (It should be noted that there are light, medium and dark shades of Gray Green.)

LIGHT YELLOW
Mask: buttercup yellow. Cheek patches: silvery white to very pale pinkish violet. General body color: back, rump, breast, flanks and underparts, deep buttercup yellow and as free from green suffusion as possible. Primaries and tail: lighter than body. Eye: black pupil with white iris.

The sulphur-crested cockatoo is one of the more common parrots to be seen in pet shops. Cockatoos are distinguished from other parrots by the crest, which can be raised and lowered. The sulphur-crested cockatoo lives in the eucalypthus forests of Australia, where it lives in flocks. Each flock has a favorite roosting tree from which they sally forth to feed. They land in clearings to eat nuts, seeds and insects; while they are feeding, sentries are left on guard to warn of approaching predators.

Opposite:
Not only the budgie is a good talker; parrots also are renowed as 'talking birds.' The parrot family includes the parrakeets, budgerigar, cockatoos, macaws (photo) and lovebirds. Most parrots live in forests, although some Australian parrots live in grassland (budgerigars!). The strong legs with curved, needle-sharp claws are excellent for climbing among branches. The sickle-shaped beak is used to help in climbing and for tearing open nuts and soft fruit, as well as being a powerful deterrent to enemies.

DARK YELLOW
Same as above but correspondingly deeper in color.

OLIVE YELLOW
As above but with a mustard body color.

GRAY YELLOW
As above but with a dull mustard body color. (It should be noted that there are light, medium and dark shades of Gray Yellow.)

SKYBLUE
Mask: clear white, ornamented by six evenly spaced large round black throat spots, the outer two being partially covered at the base by cheek patches. Cheek patches: violet. General body color: back, rump, breast flanks and underparts, pure skyblue. Markings: on cheeks, back of head, neck and wings, black and well defined on a white ground. Tail: long feathers, bluish black.

COBALT
As above but with a deep rich cobalt blue body color. Tail: long feathers, darker in proportion.

MAUVE
As above but with a purplish mauve body color with a tendency to a pinkish tone. Tail: long feathers, darker in proportion.

VIOLET
As above but with a deep intense violet body color. Tail: long feathers, darker in proportion.

GRAY
Mask: white, ornamented by six evenly spaced large round black throat spots, the outer two being partially covered at the base by cheek patches. Cheek patches: gray-blue or slate. General body color: back, rump, breast flanks and underparts, solid gray. Markings: on cheeks, back of head, neck and wings, black and well defined on a white ground. Tail: long feathers, black. (It should be noted that there are light, medium and dark shades of Gray.)

WHITE
Mask: white. General body color: back, rump, breast, flanks and underparts, white (suffused with the color being masked). Wings and tail: white, bluish or light gray. (It should be noted that there are blue, cobalt, mauve, violet and gray shades in both light and dark suffusion.)

OPALINE LIGHT GREEN

Mask: buttercup yellow, extending over back of head and merging into general body color at a point level with the butt of wings where undulations should cease thus leaving a clear V effect between top of wings so desirable in this variety, to be ornamented by six evenly spaced large round black throat spots, the outer two being partially covered at the base by cheek patches. Cheek patches: violet. General body color: mantle (including V area or saddle), back, rump, breast, flanks and underparts, bright grass green. Wings, to be the same color as body. Markings: should be normal with a suffused opalescent effect. Tail: long feathers, not to be lighter than mantle.

OPALINE SKYBLUE

As above but with a skyblue body color.

OPALINE COBALT

As above but with a cobalt body color. Tail: long feathers, not to be lighter than mantle.

OPALINE MAUVE

As above but with a mauve body color. Tail: long feathers, not to be lighter than mantle.

An Australian Dominant Pied Opaline Gray Green. This is a good bird of the right type, color, spots, and head qualities.

Left: Opaline Light Green hen. *Center:* Opaline Olive Green cock. *Right:* Normal Dark Green cock.

Head of hen   Head of cock

A cock Light Green budgerigar of good size and substance, with a Red Factor canary. Budgerigars, particularly cock birds, are generally amiable and therefore are excellent (and colorful) additions to the mixed decorative aviary.

Two budgies displaying the newest mutational adornment, the Crest. Both these birds are mature birds, and both are Green. The bird on the left is a Graywing Light Green. The other is a Normal Dark Green. The crest can be bred in three basic forms and with several variations within the confines of these forms.

OPALINE VIOLET
As above but with a deep intense violet body color. Tail: long feathers, not to be lighter than mantle.

OPALINE GRAY
As above but with a solid gray body color. Cheek patches: gray to slate. Tail: long feathers, no lighter than mantle. (It should be noted that there are light, medium and dark shades of Opaline Gray.)

OPALINE WHITE
As for White but with a suggestion of Opaline characteristics.

OPALINE YELLOW
As for Yellow but with a suggestion of Opaline characteristics.

OPALINE CINNAMON LIGHT GREEN
Mask: buttercup yellow, extending over back of head and merging into general body color at a point level with butt of wings where undulations should cease, thus leaving a clear V effect between top of wings so desirable in this variety, to be ornamented by six evenly spaced large cinnamon brown throat spots; the outer two being partially covered at the base by cheek patches. Cheek patches: violet. General body color: mantle (including V area or saddle), back, rump, breast, flanks and underparts, pale grass green. Wings to be same color as body. Markings: should be normal cinnamon brown with a suffused opalescent effect. Tail: long feathers, not to be lighter than mantle.

OPALINE CINNAMON DARK GREEN
As above but with a light laurel green body color. Tail: long feathers, not to be lighter than mantle.

OPALINE CINNAMON OLIVE GREEN
As above but with a light olive green body color. Tail: long feathers, not to be lighter than mantle.

OPALINE CINNAMON GRAY GREEN
As above but with a pale gray green body color. Tail: long feathers, not to be lighter than mantle. Cheek patches: gray to slate. (It should be noted that there are light, medium and dark shades of Opaline Cinnamon Gray Green.)

OPALINE CINNAMON SKYBLUE
Mask: white, extending over back of head and merging into general body color at a point level with butt of wings where undulations

should cease, thus leaving a clear V effect between top of wings so desirable in this variety; to be ornamented by six evenly spaced large round cinnamon brown throat spots, the outer two being partially covered at the base by cheek patches. Cheek patches: violet. General body color: mantle, back, rump, breast, flanks and underparts, pale skyblue. Markings: should be normal cinnamon brown on pale blue ground with suffused opalescent effect. Tail: long feathers, not to be lighter than mantle.

OPALINE CINNAMON COBALT
As above but with pale cobalt body color. Tail: long feathers, not to be lighter than mantle.

OPALINE CINNAMON MAUVE
As above but with pale mauve body color. Tail: long feathers, not to be lighter than mantle.

OPALINE CINNAMON GRAY
As above but with pale gray body color. Cheek patches: gray to slate. Tail: long feathers, not to be lighter than mantle. (It should be noted that there are light, medium and dark shades of Opaline Cinnamon Gray.)

CINNAMON LIGHT GREEN
Mask: buttercup yellow, ornamented by six evenly spaced large round cinnamon brown throat spots, the outer two being partially covered at the base by cheek patches. Cheek patches: violet. General body color: back, rump, breast, flanks and underparts grass green, 50 per cent or more of normal body color. Markings: on cheeks, back of head, neck and wings, cinnamon brown on a yellow ground and distinct as in normal color. Tail: long feathers, dark blue with brown quill.

CINNAMON DARK GREEN
As above but with a light laurel green body color. Tail: long feathers, darker in proportion.

CINNAMON OLIVE GREEN
As above but with a light olive green body color. Tail: long feathers, darker in proportion.

CINNAMON GRAY GREEN
As above but with a pale gray green body color. Cheek patches: gray to slate. Tail: long feathers, of a deep cinnamon shade. (It should be noted that there are light, medium and dark shades of Cinnamon Gray Green.)

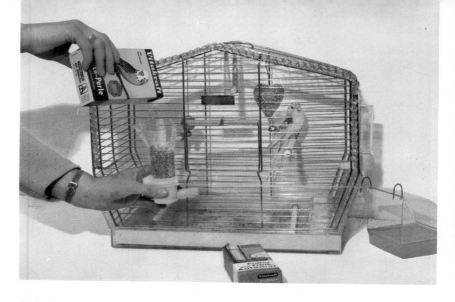

It is important to feed a newly purchased bird the same mixture he is used to. Different breeders and dealers feed slightly varying amounts of each kind of seed. A popular mixture is: four parts large canary seed, two parts white Proso millet and one part oats. A bird at first cannot find the seeds in the cup.

Opposite:
Above: This special type of nest box, larger than the common type, has the exit hole set off center, not because the hen or cock will break the eggs by coming down directly onto them, but so that the young, clumsy chicks, going in and out of the box, will not break second-clutch eggs as they descend into the nest box. Nest boxes should not be too shallow in depth, for this makes it too easy for vigorous, inquisitive chicks to leave the nest box too early. **Below:** The nest boxes can be inspected occasionally while the budgies are still incubating to see whether things are going smoothly on their natural course.

CINNAMON SKYBLUE
Mask: white, ornamented by six evenly spaced large round cinnamon brown throat spots, the outer two being partially covered at the base by cheek patches. Cheek patches: violet. General body color: back, rump, breast, flanks and underparts skyblue, 50 per cent or more of normal body color. Markings: cheeks, back of head, neck and wings cinnamon brown on white ground and distinct as in normal color. Tail: long feathers, blue with brown quill.

CINNAMON COBALT
As above but with pale cobalt body color. Tail: long feathers, cobalt with cinnamon shade.

CINNAMON MAUVE
As above but with pale mauve body color. Tail: long feathers, mauve with cinnamon shade.

CINNAMON VIOLET
As above but with pale violet body color. Tail: long feathers, violet with cinnamon shade.

CINNAMON GRAY
As above but with pale gray body color. Cheek patches: pale gray. Tail: long feathers, pale gray with cinnamon shade. (It should be noted that there are light, medium and dark shades of Cinnamon Gray.)

GRAYWING LIGHT GREEN
Mask: yellow, ornamented by six evenly spaced large round gray throat spots, the outer two being partially covered at the base by cheek patches. Cheek patches: pale violet. General body color: back, rump, breast, flanks and underparts grass green, 50 per cent or more of normal body color. Markings: on cheek, back of head, neck and wings should be light gray and distinct as in normal color. Tail: long feathers, gray with pale bluish tinge.

GRAYWING DARK GREEN
As above but with a light laurel green body color. Tail: long feathers, darker in proportion.

GRAYWING OLIVE GREEN
As above but with a light olive green body color. Tail: long feathers, darker in proportion.

GRAYWING GRAY GREEN
As above but with a light mustard green body color. Cheek patches: light gray. Tail: long feathers, dark gray. (It should be noted that there are light, medium and dark shades of Graywing Gray Green.)

GRAYWING SKYBLUE
Mask: white, ornamented by six evenly spaced large round gray throat spots, the outer two being partially covered at the base by cheek patches. Cheek patches: light violet. General body color: back, rump, breast, flanks and underparts skyblue, 50 per cent or more of normal body color. Markings: on cheek, back of head, neck and wings should be light gray and distinct as in normal color. Tail: long feathers, grayish blue tinge.

GRAYWING COBALT
As above but with a pale cobalt body color. Tail: long feathers, darker in proportion.

GRAYWING MAUVE
As above but with a pale mauve body color. Tail: long feathers, darker in proportion.

GRAYWING VIOLET
As above but with a pale violet body color. Tail: long feathers, darker in proportion.

GRAYWING GRAY
As above but with a pale gray body color. Cheek patches: pale gray. Tail: long feathers, dark gray. (It should be noted that there are light, medium and dark shades of Graywing Gray.)

OPALINE GRAYWING LIGHT GREEN
Mask: yellow, extending over back of head and merging into general body color at a point level with butt of wings where undulations should cease, leaving a definite V effect between top of wings so desirable in this variety, to be ornamented by six evenly spaced large round gray throat spots, the outer two being partially covered at the base by cheek patches. Cheek patches: violet. General body color: mantle (including V area or saddle), back, rump, breast, flanks and underparts, pale grass green. Wings same color as body. Markings: should be normal and light gray in color with suffused opalescent effect. Tail: long feathers, smoky gray.

Because of the many mutations in color and pattern, the budgie is one of the most variegated and beautiful of birds. Breeders, quick to recognize new phases, have increased the budgie's optical fascination by selecting for and breeding them in a rainbow of brilliant colors. Above are examples of the basic Green budgie (on the left), a Cobalt Normal, a Gray Normal, and an Opaline Light Green.

Opposite:
With its gaudy but beautiful plumage, the blue and yellow macaw, an inhabitant of South American forests, is a favorite in zoos and pet shops. Its flight, with slow shallow wingbeats and long tail streaming behind, is surprisingly fast. There is no reason why budgie fanciers can't have a macaw as well also; they make wonderful pets and are a delight to everybody.

OPALINE GRAYWING DARK GREEN
As above but with a light laurel green body color. Tail: long feathers, darker in proportion.

OPALINE GRAYWING OLIVE GREEN
As above but with a light olive green body color. Tail: long feathers, darker in proportion.

OPALINE GRAYWING GRAY GREEN
As above but with a light mustard body color. Cheek patches: light gray. Tail: long feathers, dark gray. (It should be noted that there are light, medium and dark shades of Opaline Graywing Gray Green.)

OPALINE GRAYWING SKYBLUE
Mask: white, extending over back of head and merging into general body color at a point level with the butt of wings where undulations should cease, leaving a definite clear V effect between top of wings, so desirable in this variety, to be ornamented by six evenly spaced large round gray throat spots, the outer two being partially covered at the base by cheek patches. Cheek patches: violet. General body color: mantle (including V area or saddle), back, rump, breast, flanks and underparts, pale skyblue. Wings same color as body. Markings: should be normal and gray in color with suffused opalescent effect. Tail: long feathers, gray.

OPALINE GRAYWING COBALT
As above but with pale cobalt body color. Tail: darker in proportion.

OPALINE GRAYWING MAUVE
As above but with pale mauve body color. Tail: darker in proportion.

OPALINE GRAYWING VIOLET
As above but with pale violet body color. Tail: darker in proportion.

OPALINE GRAYWING GRAY
As above but with pale gray body color. Cheek patches: light gray. Tail: long feathers, gray. (It should be noted that there are light, medium and dark shades of Opaline Graywing Gray.)

YELLOW-WING LIGHT GREEN
Mask: buttercup yellow. Cheek patches: violet. General body color: back, rump, breast, flanks and underparts, bright grass green. Wings: buttercup yellow, as free from markings as possible. Tail: long feathers, bluish. (*Note:* Clearwings showing opaline characteristics should be shown in the A.O.C. or V. class.)

YELLOW-WING DARK GREEN
As above but with dark laurel green body color. Tail: long feathers, darker in proportion.

YELLOW-WING OLIVE GREEN
As above but with an olive green body color. Tail: long feathers, darker in proportion.

YELLOW-WING GRAY GREEN
This variety conforms to the standard of Yellow-wing Light Green except that general body color should be dull mustard green. Cheek patches: gray to slate. Tail: long feathers, darker in proportion. (It should be noted that there are light, medium and dark shades of Yellow-wing Gray Green.)

WHITEWING SKYBLUE
Mask: white. Cheek patches: violet. General body color: back, rump, breast, flanks and underparts, pure skyblue approximating to the normal variety. Wings: white, as free from markings as possible. Tail: long feathers, bluish. (*Note:* Clearwings showing opaline characteristics should be shown in the A.O.C. or V class.)

WHITEWING COBALT
As above but with a cobalt body color. Tail: long feathers, darker in proportion.

WHITEWING MAUVE
As above but with a mauve body color. Tail: long feathers, darker in proportion.

WHITEWING VIOLET
As above but with a violet body color. Tail: long feathers, darker in proportion.

WHITEWING GRAY
As above but with a gray body color. Cheek patches: gray-blue. Tail: long feathers, gray. (It should be noted that there are light, medium and dark shades of Whitewing Gray.)

FALLOW LIGHT GREEN
Mask: yellow, ornamented by six evenly spaced large round brown throat spots, the outer two being partially covered at the base by cheek patches. Cheek patches: violet. General body color: back, rump, breast, flanks and underparts, yellowish green. Markings: on cheeks, back of head, neck and wings, medium brown on a yellow

Petz's conure. Petz's conure is more popularly known in the United States as the halfmoon conure and is sold mainly as a pet "dwarf parrot." Sexes are particularly difficult to determine. A good pet halfmoon is really a delightful bird, and youngsters are reasonably easy to train. Keeping them with budgies in an aviary is possible, and it gives color and variety to the collection!

Senegal parrots are relatively inexpensive and have a reputation for being charming pets. They are very docile and are among the hardiest of parrots; given a chance, they will thrive for many years, never giving their owners trouble and worry by being sick. If you have experience in keeping and breeding budgies, perhaps this species should be your next step———they're worth it!

ground. Eyes: red or plum. Tail: long feathers, bluish gray.

FALLOW DARK GREEN
As above but with a light laurel green body color. Tail: long feathers, darker in proportion.

FALLOW OLIVE GREEN
As above but with a light mustard olive green body color. Tail: long feathers, darker in proportion.

FALLOW SKYBLUE
Mask: white, ornamented by six evenly spaced large round brown throat spots, the outer two being partially covered at base by cheek patches. Cheek patches: violet. General body color: back, rump, breast, flanks and underparts, pale skyblue. Markings: on cheeks, back of head, neck and wings, medium brown on a white ground. Eyes: red or plum. Tail: long feathers, bluish gray.

FALLOW COBALT
As above but with a warm cobalt body color. Tail: long feathers, darker in proportion.

FALLOW MAUVE
As above but with a pale mauve body color of a pinkish tone. Tail: long feathers, darker in proportion.

FALLOW VIOLET
As above but with a pale violet body color. Tail: long feathers, darker in proportion.

FALLOW GRAY
As above but with a pale gray body color. Cheek patches: gray to slate. Tail: long feathers, darker in proportion. (It should be noted that there are light, medium and dark shades of Fallow Gray.) English and German forms are recognized: the German form having a white iris ring around the eye, the English form has none.

LUTINO
Buttercup yellow throughout. Eye: clear red. Cheek patches: silvery white. Tail: long feathers and primaries yellowish white.

ALBINO
White throughout. Eyes: clear red.

YELLOW-FACE
All varieties in the blue series except Pieds. Mask: yellow only, other-

wise exactly as corresponding normal variety. *Note:* yellow-marked feathers in tail permissible.

Pieds

DOMINANT PIED LIGHT GREEN

Mask: buttercup yellow of an even tone, ornamented by six evenly spaced and clearly defined large round black throat spots, the outer two being partially covered at the base by cheek patches. Cheek patches: violet. General body color: as the normal Light Green variety but broken with irregular patches of clear buttercup yellow or with a clear yellow band approximately ½ in. wide round its middle just above the thighs. An all yellow or normal green colored body should be penalized. Head patch is optional. (*Note:* all other things being equal, preference to be given, in accordance with the scale of show points, to birds showing the band.) Wings: color and markings as the normal Light Green but having irregular patches of clear buttercup yellow or with part of the wing edges to shoulder butt clear yellow on an otherwise normal marked wing. Completely clear wings should be penalized. Wing markings may be grizzled in appearance. All visible flight feathers should be clear yellow but odd dark flight feathers are not faults. Tail: the two long tail feathers may be clear yellow, marked or normal blue-black in color. Cere: similar to that of the normal Light Green or a mixture of normal color and fleshy pink. Eyes: dark with light iris ring. Beak: normal horn color. Feed and legs: blue mottled as the normal Light Green, fleshy pink or a mixture of both.

DOMINANT PIED DARK GREEN

As above but with general body color as for normal Dark Green.

DOMINANT PIED OLIVE GREEN

As above but with general body color as for normal Olive Green.

DOMINANT PIED GRAY GREEN

As above but with general body color as for normal Gray Green. Cheek patches: gray-blue to slate. (It should be noted that there are light, medium and dark shades of Dominant Pied Gray Green.)

DOMINANT PIED SKYBLUE

Mask: white, ornamented by six evenly spaced and clearly defined large round black throat spots, the outer two being partially covered at the base by cheek patches. Cheek patches: violet. General body color: as the normal Skyblue variety but broken with irregular patches of white or with a clear white band approximately ½ in. wide round its middle just above the thighs. An all-white or normal blue colored body should be penalized. Head patch is optional (*Note:* all

A step up from keeping and breeding budgerigars is the keeping and breeding of Australian parrakeets. The rock pebbler *(Polytelis anthopeplus)* is a very hardy bird. It will breed well in an outdoor aviary if the flight is quiet and long. A pair needs a deep nest box with some rotted wood on the bottom. This wood will be chewed up by the birds to a moist bed on which the hen will lay four eggs.

The Cloncurry parrakeet is rare in captivity. Sexes are similar, but the hens are slightly less vivid and have a smaller head and bill. Immatures have a frontal orange band. Some serious aviculturists have been very successful in breeding it.

Peach faced love birds (*Agapornis roseicollis*) are easy to breed, just like budgerigars. Very few parrot family birds build nests, and none go through such elaborate and amusing preparations with the nesting materials as do these beautiful lovebirds. They first cut it into long strips and then soften it with their beaks before tucking it between feathers on sides and rump for the flight to the nest box. Much of the material becomes dislodged during the flight to the nest and falls to the ground. The nest of this species is primitive compared to the nests of other lovebirds, especially those of the white eye-ringed species which carry nesting materials in their beaks.

other things being equal, preference to be given, in accordance with the scale of show points, to birds showing the band.) Wings: color and markings as the normal Skyblue but having irregular patches of clear white or with part of the wing edges to shoulder butt clear white on an otherwise normal marked wing. Completely clear wings should be penalized. Wing markings may be grizzled in appearance. All visible flight feathers should be clear white but odd dark feathers are not faults. Tail: the two long tail feathers may be clear white, marked or normal blue-black in color. Cere: similar to that of normal Skyblue or a mixture of normal color and fleshy pink. Eyes: dark with light iris ring. Beak: normal horn color. Feet and legs: blue mottled as the normal Skyblue, fleshy pink or mixture of both.

DOMINANT PIED COBALT
As above but with general body color as for normal Cobalt.

DOMINANT PIED MAUVE
As above but with general body color as for normal Mauve.

DOMINANT PIED VIOLET
As above but with general body color as for normal Violet.

DOMINANT PIED GRAY
As above but with general body color as for normal Gray. Cheek patches: gray-blue or slate. (It should be noted that there are light, medium and dark shades of Dominant Pied Gray.) *Note:* an Opaline, Yellow-face and Cinnamon form of Dominant Pied is recognized but these should only be shown in Dominant Pied classes.

CLEARFLIGHT LIGHT GREEN
Mask: buttercup yellow of an even color ornamented by six evenly spaced clearly defined large round black throat spots, the outer two being partially covered at the base by the cheek patches. Cheek patches: violet. General body color: as the normal Light Green with the exception of one small patch approximately one-half in. by five-eighths in. of clear buttercup yellow at the back of the head. Slight collar or extension of the bib, while undesirable, will not penalize. Wings: color and markings as the normal Light Green but with seven visible flight feathers of clear yellow. Dark flights constitute a fault. Tail: the two long feathers should be clear yellow, dark tail feathers are a fault. Cere: similar to that of normal Light Green. Eyes: dark with light iris ring. Beak: normal horn color. Feet and legs: blue mottled or flesh colored.

CLEARFLIGHT DARK GREEN
As above but with general body color as for normal Dark Green.

CLEARFLIGHT OLIVE GREEN
As above but with general body color as for normal Olive Green.

CLEARFLIGHT GREY GREEN
As above but with general body color as for normal Gray Green. Cheek patches: gray-blue or slate. (It should be noted that there are light, medium and dark shades of Pied (clear flighted) Gray Green.)

CLEARFLIGHT SKYBLUE
Mask: white, ornamented by six evenly spaced clearly defined large round black throat spots, the outer two being partially covered at the base by cheek patches. Cheek patches: violet. General body color: as the normal Skyblue with the exception of one small approximately one-half in. by five-eighths in. of pure white at the back of the head. Slight collar or extension of bib, while undesirable, will not penalize. Wings: as normal Skyblue but with seven visible flight feathers of pure white. Dark flights constitute a fault. Tail: the two long feathers should be pure white, marked or dark tail feathers are a fault. Cere: similar to that of normal Skyblue. Eyes: dark with light iris ring. Beak: normal horn color. Feet and legs: bluish mottled or flesh color.

CLEARFLIGHT COBALT
As above but with general body as for normal Cobalt.

CLEARFLIGHT MAUVE
As above but with general body color as for normal Mauve.

CLEARFLIGHT VIOLET
As above but with general body color as for normal Violet.

CLEARFLIGHT GREY
As above but with general body color as for normal Gray. Cheek patches: gray-blue to slate. (It should be noted that there are light, medium and dark shades of Clearflight Gray.) *Note:* An Opaline, Yellow-face and Cinnamon form of Clearflights is recognized but these should only be shown in Clearflight classes. The non-head-spot type of Clearflight (described as Australian) with full body color is recognized and should be exhibited in Clearflight classes where these are provided.

DARK-EYED CLEAR YELLOW
Cheek patches: silvery-white. General body color: pure yellow throughout and free from any odd green feathers or green suffusion. Wings: pure yellow throughout, free from black or grizzled tickings or green suffusion. All flight feathers paler yellow than rump color. Tail: as the flight feathers. Cere: fleshy pink in color as in Lutinos. Eyes:

The Tui Parrot (*Brotogeris s. sanctithoma*) is probably the prettiest of all the *Brotogeris* species. Tui parrots may be kept with other parrakeets provided they are not of related species. It is quite possible to obtain breeding results.

Opposite:
The redrump parrakeet (*Psephotus haematonotus*) is from south and southeast Australia and very easy to breed, even when kept in large aviaries with other birds (budgerigars), but not with their own kind. The first breeding results were reported in Britain in 1863. Crossings with the rosella and the Stanley parrakeet are on record.

dark without any light iris rings. Beak: orange colored. Feet and legs: fleshy pink. (*Note:* the actual body color varies in depth according to the genetic makeup, i.e. whether light, dark or olive green, etc.)

DARK-EYED CLEAR WHITE

As above but with white body color and free from any blue suffusion or odd blue feathers. Flights and tail: white. Cere: fleshy pink in color as in Albinos. (*Note:* a dominant form is also recognized having normal cere, eyes, beak, feet and legs, which may be exhibited with the above-mentioned types of dark-eyed yellow and/or whites where separate classes are scheduled for this variety. A yellow-faced form of dark-eyed clear is also recognized but should only be shown in Dark-eyed Clear classes.)

RECESSIVE PIED LIGHT GREEN

Mask: buttercup yellow of an even tone. Throat spots: as the normal Light Green variety; may be present from one to full number. Cheek patches: violet, silvery-white or a mixture of both. General body color: irregular patches of clear buttercup yellow and bright grass green with the latter mainly on the lower chest, rump and underparts. Zebra markings on the top of the head and around the eyes are not faults. Wings: black undulations or polka-dot markings should not cover more than fifteen to twenty per cent of total area. All visible flight feathers should be clear yellow but odd dark flight feathers are not faults. Cere: fleshy pink in color as in Lutinos. Eyes: dark without any light iris ring: Beak: orange colored. Feet and legs: fleshy pink.

RECESSIVE PIED DARK GREEN

As above with a yellow and dark green body color.

RECESSIVE PIED OLIVE GREEN

As above but with a yellow and olive green body color.

RECESSIVE PIED GRAY GREEN

As above but with a yellow and gray-green body color. Cheek patches: gray-blue or slate, or a mixture of both. (It should be noted that there are light, medium and dark shades of Recessive Pied Gray Green.)

RECESSIVE PIED SKYBLUE

Mask: white. Throat spots: as the normal Skyblue variety; may be present from one to full number. Cheek patches: violet, silvery-white or a mixture of both. General body color: irregular patches of white and bright skyblue with the latter mainly on the lower chest, rump and underparts. Zebra markings on top of head and around the eyes are not faults. Wings: black undulations or polka-dot markings should not cover more than fifteen to twenty per cent of total area. All visible flight feathers should be white but odd dark flight feathers are not faults. Cere: fleshy pink in color as in Albinos. Eyes: dark without any light iris ring. Beak: orange colored. Feet and legs: fleshy pink.

RECESSIVE PIED COBALT
As above but with a white and cobalt body color.

RECESSIVE PIED MAUVE
As above but with a white and mauve body color.

RECESSIVE PIED VIOLET
As above but with a white and violet body color.

RECESSIVE PIED GRAY
As above but with a white and gray body color. Cheek patches: gray-blue or slate, or a mixture of both. (It should be noted that there are light, medium and dark forms of Recessive Pied Gray). *Note:* Opaline, Yellow-face and Cinnamon forms of Recessive Pied are recognized but these should be shown only in Recessive Pied classes.

LACEWING YELLOW
Mask: yellow, ornamented by six evenly spaced large round cinnamon throat spots, the outer two being partially covered at the base by cheek patches. Cheek patches: pale violet. General body color: back, rump, breast, flanks and underparts, yellow. Markings: on cheeks, back of head, neck, mantle and wings, cinnamon brown on a yellow ground. Eyes: clear with light iris rings. Tail: long feathers, cinnamon brown. *Note:* the depth of yellow of the body color, etc. varies according to the normal counterpart being masked by the Lacewing character, i.e. the richest yellow is carried by the Lacewing Olive Green and the lightest by the Lacewing Light Green.

LACEWING WHITE
Mask: white, ornamented by six evenly spaced large round cinnamon throat spots, the outer two being partially covered at the base by cheek patches. Cheek patches: pale violet. General body color: back, rump, breast, flanks and underparts, white. Markings: on cheeks, back of head, neck, mantle and wings, cinnamon brown on a white ground. Eyes: clear red with light iris rings. Tail: long feathers, cinnamon brown. *Note:* the shade of white of the body color, etc. varies only slightly in tone according to the normal counterpart being masked by the lacewing character. (A Yellow-faced form is recognized. Where no classes are scheduled for this variety it should be shown in any other color classes.)

Budgerigars are unique in their method of raising a nest of young. They produce a type of milk in their crops which is used as the sole food for newly hatched and small young. This crop or budgie "milk" is similar in composition to pigeon "milk," the substance with which parent pigeons feed their young. It consists of fats and proteins and is semi-liquid. The quality of this budgie milk is greatly improved if budgerigars are supplied with a soft food containing animal proteins when they are feeding young. Experience has taught that minor food deficiencies and resulting feather troubles are avoided in this way. Wild birds of the small seed-eating varieties consume large quantities of insects (animal proteins) while feeding young, and it seems reasonable to assume that budgerigars are not an exception. When adult birds start to feed each other, they are both in breeding condition.

The Violet (left) can be bred in the visual form, true violet, and in two so-called non-visual forms, Sky Violet and Mauve Violet. The Sky Violet looks very much like a Cobalt, and the Mauve Violet generally has the appearance of any other Mauve. In most cases the true color characteristics of the Sky Violet (a no-dark-factor bird) and the Mauve Violet (a two-dark-factor bird) can only be ascertained by breeding results. The Light Green (right) color is, like all other Green colors, dominant to all other colors. Breed a pure green to any other color and the young resulting from the mating will be green in color, but split (carrying a recessive) to produce the partner color when mated to a bird of the partner series.

The budgerigar, though appearing in many different colors, has never been crossed with any other species. All the colors we have today have been bred from the original wild type budgerigar which is light green. Any color may be crossed with another since these birds, though able to distinguish color, do not hesitate to mate with any shade of their own species.

Color breeding is fascinating, but it should be done with a definite plan in mind. To mate different colors without a very good reason is not recommended. The Light Green is the original and never needs to be crossed with other colors to improve its shading. Some colors occasionally need to be crossed with a lighter or darker shade to keep the color rich and lustrous or to obtain a desired shade. Haphazard crossing of various colors is apt to lead to faded, patchy or muddy looking specimens and to too many white young in nests from dark parents.

The Light Green

There are purebred Light Greens, not split to any other color, and Green/blues, Green/yellows and Green/whites. The Green/whites are also split to blue and yellow. Two Green/white parents will produce green, blue, and white young with the Greens predominating. Normal Greens may also be split to the rare colors and cocks may be split to the sex-linked varieties.

The following are a few matings:

Light Green x Light Green =	100% Light Green
Light Green x Dark Green =	50% Light Green 50% Dark Green
Light Green x Olive Green =	100% Dark Green
Light Green x Sky Blue =	100% Light Green/Blue
Light Green x Cobalt =	50% Light Green/Blue 50% Dark Green/Blue
Light Green x Mauve =	100% Dark Green/Blue

Light Green x Light Yellow =	100% Light Green/Yellow
Light Green x Dark Yellow =	50% Light Green/Yellow 50% Dark Green/Yellow
Light Green x Olive Yellow =	100% Dark Green/Yellow
Light Green x Light Green/Blue =	50% Light Green 50% Light Green/Blue
Light Green x Dark Green/Blue =	25% Light Green 25% Dark Green 25% Light Green/Blue 25% Dark Green/Blue
Light Green x Olive Green/Blue =	50% Dark Green 50% Dark Green/Blue
Light Green x Light Green/Yellow =	50% Light Green 50% Light Green/Yellow
Light Green x Dark Green/Yellow =	25% Light Green 25% Dark Green 25% Light Green/Yellow 25% Dark Green/Yellow
Light Green x Olive Green/Yellow =	50% Dark Green 50% Dark Green/Yellow
Light Green x Light Green/White =	25% Light Green 25% Light Green/Blue 25% Light Green/Yellow 25% Light Green/White

The Dark Green

This mutation occurred in 1915 and is very popular with breeders as well as with the pet-loving public. It is of a shade between the Light Green and the Olive Green and the mask shows a deeper yellow than seen in the Light Green. The Dark Green budgerigar is not a purebred bird; it is a cross and will always remain one. It is used for the production of deeply colored Cobalts and Sky Blues of a rich shade. When an Olive Green is mated with a Light Green, all young will be Dark Green. Dark Green/blues may be produced by mating Light Green x Cobalt =

50% Light Green/blue
50% Dark Green/blue

Light Green x Mauve=   100% Dark Green/blue

Bourke's (pair farther from nest box) and redrump parrakeets are also very popular Australian birds, but keeping them with budgies in the same aviary is not

advisable. They don't need a large aviary, and any budgie-fancier can try his luck with these very popular and beautiful parrakeets—especially after he has a lot of experience with budgies.

The budgerigar, *Melopsittacus undulatus*, is the best known of the 52 psittacines from Australia. The birds inhabit the arid interior. These are wild birds.

At the present time the keeping and breeding of budgerigars in cages and aviaries is practiced most extensively by fanciers all over the world.

Light Green/blue x Cobalt = 25% Light Green/blue
25% Dark Green/blue
25% Cobalt
25% Sky Blue

Olive Green x Sky Blue = 100% Dark Green/blue

Dark Greens are valuable for producing Olive Greens.
A few matings:

Dark Green x Light Green = 50% Light Green
50% Dark Green

Dark Green x Dark Green = 33⅓% Light Green,
33⅓% Dark Green
33⅓ % Olive Green

Dark Green/Cobalt x Olive Green = 50% Light Green/Blue
50% Dark Green/Blue

Dark Green x Cobalt = 33⅓% Light Green/Blue,
33⅓% Dark Green/Blue
33⅓% Olive Green/Blue

Dark Green x Mavue = 50% Dark Green/Blue
50% Olive Green/Blue

Dark Green x Light Yellow = 50% Light Green/Yellow
50% Dark Green/Yellow

Dark Green x Dark Yellow = 33⅓% Light Green/Yellow,
33⅓% Dark Green/Yellow
33⅓% Olive Green/Yellow

Dark Green x Olive Yellow = 50% Dark Green/Yellow
50% Olive Green/Yellow

Dark Green x Light Green/Blue = 25% Light Green,
25% Dark Green
25% Light Green/Blue
25% Dark Green/Blue

Dark Green x Olive Green/Blue = 25% Dark Green
25% Olive Green
25% Dark Green/Blue
25% Olive Green/Blue

Dark Green x Light Green/Yellow = 25% Light Green
25 % Dark Green
25 % Light Green/Yellow
25 % Dark Green/Yellow

Dark Green x Dark Green/Yellow =   Light Green, Dark Green
Olive Green, Light Green/Yellow
Dark Green/Yellow
Olive Green/Yellow

Dark Green x Olive Green/Yellow =   25% Dark Green
25% Olive Green
25% Dark Green/Yellow
25% Olive Green/Yellow

Dark Green x Light Yellow/White =   25% Light Green/Yellow
25% Dark Green/Yellow
25% Light Green/White
25% Dark Green/White

The Olive Green

The darkest color variety of the green series is the Olive. For pets it may not be as popular as the more brilliant colors but the shade is one of the most valuable to the color breeder.

Its first appearance dates back to 1916 when a specimen was bred by the French breeder M. Blanchard in Toulouse. Soon more budgerigars of this shade were bred in Europe. It is now used for cross-breeding with other colors to achieve certain effects, especially to deepen the color of Cobalts and Mauves.

Olive budgerigars for the show bench should be bred pure. The mating of Olive to Olive gives the best results for this purpose. Olives split to other colors are often patchy in appearance or show an undesirable green tint. After breeding Olives pure for some generations, it may be found necessary to outcross to another color such as Mauve, Yellow Olive, or Cinnamon to preserve strength and size while improving color. The olive variety has given us several new colors by mutation and it is possible that some day it may produce a black, or near black, budgerigar.

Breeders who are interested in odd colors will keep their eyes on the Olive Green. Crossed with Cinnamon it produces the Cinnamon Olive, a bird of a beautiful bronze shade. The Opaline Olive and the Fallow Olive may be produced by suitable matings. These varieties show the olive breast color in a lighter shade, varying

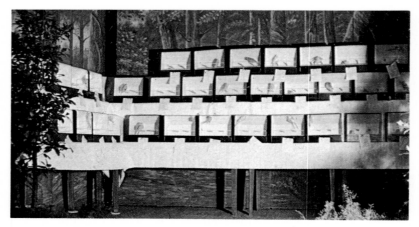

Scenes from budgie exhibitions. There are certain qualities which budgerigars must possess before they can gain prizes in competition on the show bench. Quite a lot of training and preparation are needed before the budgerigars are in a suitable state for going to a show.

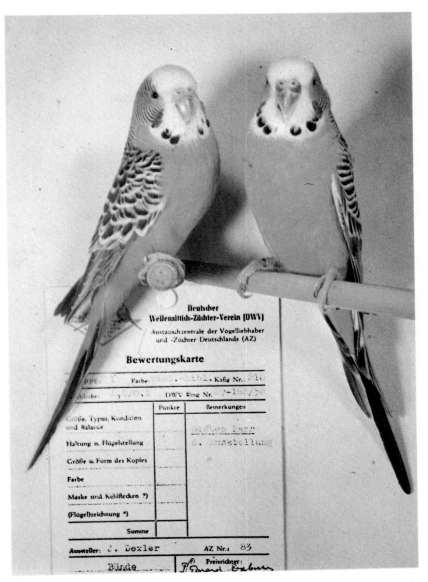

Budgerigars are the most popular of all caged birds and have much to recommend them as show birds, as they take kindly to cage life, they are reasonably easy to train and they are to be had in such a wonderful range of beautifully colored varieties.

according to the color with which they are crossed. Even the Olive Graywing, easily produced in the first generation by crossing with Graywing Dark Green, or in the second generation by crossing with Graywing Light Green, is an attractive bird. The somber normal olive color on the breast will be diluted to a more pleasing lighter hue. All of these colors are in demand as pets by those who prefer the unusual.

The following are a few matings which will produce Olives:

Dark Green x Mauve =

50% Olive/blue
50% Dark Green/blue

Dark Green/blue x Mauve =

50% Olive/blue
50% deep Cobalt

Olive/blue x Mauve =

50% Olive/blue
50% Mauve

Olive x Mauve =   100% Olive/blue

Olive/blue x Olive/blue =

25% pure Olive
50% Olive/blue
25% Mauve

Olive x Olive =   100% Olive

When mating two Olive/blues, the resulting pure Olives may be separated from the Olive/blues by examining the young on the under side before their first molt. The Olive/blues show a definite bluish suffusion toward the vent. This will disappear when adult feathers have grown.

The Yellow
Yellow budgerigars come in three varieties just as do the Green (the Light Green, the Dark Green, and

the Olive Green). These are known as the Light Yellow, the Dark Yellow and the Olive Yellow. Each has been bred in a number of different shades.

The common Light Yellows vary greatly. There are those which show a grass green suffusion on breast and rump, faint in some specimens, deeper in others. They are pretty birds and very desirable as pets, but they are not what the show bird breeder calls a "good" Yellow. These common Yellows are frequently called Chartreuse on account of their decided green suffusion.

Show standards demand that the bird should be as free of any green as possible. Almost pure yellow budgerigars, called Buttercup, have been bred. They are handsome birds with black eyes. The quickest way to get started on the production of Buttercup Yellows is to purchase breeding stock of this color. It is possible to produce this variety by selecting the purest Yellows from a group of common Yellows with faint green suffusion, but this is a slow process.

Buttercup Yellows should not be crossed with other colors, as the pure yellow shade will be lost. From a good strain of these birds most of the genes carrying the factor for green suffusion have been eliminated. If Greens or suffused Yellows are introduced into a strain of Buttercup Yellows, undesirable genes will ruin all the work of building up a good strain of pure Yellows. When a strain of Buttercup Yellows shows signs of weakening, the breeder should shop carefully for another bird of the same pure appearance and ancestry and use only such a bird to bring new blood into his old strain.

Similarly, the Dark Yellows should not show much green suffusion, just deep yellow color. Olive Yellows of good quality are very rare. Some birds of this shade are of a muddy appearance and not attractive. But with proper selection and carefully controlled ancestry a beautiful and unusual color may be developed.

The idea hen budgerigar. Note specifically the shape of the skull and the cere. In females, even in the nest, the cere is less prominent and less fully lobed; it also is flatter and less pink than in the mates.

Yellows may be split white. If any Whites appear in a nest of yellow parents, both parents are split white. Whites bred from Olive Yellows usually show a deep blue suffusion. A breeder who wants this blue tint should use Olive Yellow/white to secure it.

Following are a few matings that will produce Dark yellows, which in turn are used for Olive Yellow production:

Dark Green/yellow x Light Yellow =
> 25% Dark Green/yellow
> 25% Light Green/yellow
> 25% Dark Yellow
> 25% Light Yellow

Mauve/white x Light Yellow =
> 50% Dark Green/white
> 50% Dark Yellow/white

Dark Yellow x Dark Yellow =
> 25% Light Yellow
> 50% Dark Yellow
> 25% Olive Yellow

Olive Yellow x Olive Yellow = 100% Olive Yellow

A novice breeder should realize that there is a great difference between an Olive Yellow and an Olive/-yellow. The former is a pure Yellow with olive suffusion, while the latter is an Olive which looks like any other Olive, but has the capacity to produce yellow birds when mated to Yellow (called Olive split yellow).

Yellows were seen among wild flocks of budgerigars in Australia and later appeared in captivity about 1875.

The Sky Blue
This color is one of those most admired by bird lovers. It made its first appearance in Europe around 1880. It is hard to understand now, when we have an abundance of blue budgerigars at our disposal, what

excitement the first specimens of this color caused. The first ones on record were bred in Belgium and Germany but disappeared again. Thirty years later, in 1910, the English "Avicultural Magazine" published a report of an exhibition of Blues at the London Cage Bird Association show.

Two sky blue budgerigars will produce all sky blue young unless split white, in which case twenty-five percent of the young will be white with a sky blue suffusion. The Sky Blues are also called Azure or Turquoise. They may be bred together for some generations, but in order to preserve the rich luster of the blue color, an occasional cross with Green is advisable. The resulting Green/blues are as a rule large, powerful birds, highly prized possessions in any aviary. Light Green/blue bred back to Blue will produce fifty percent Light Green/blues and fifty percent Sky Blues of a good turquoise shade. The Dark Green may also be used for outcrossing purposes.

A few matings:

Sky Blue x Light Green =	100% Light Green/Blue
Sky Blue x Dark Green =	50% Light Green/Blue
	50% Dark Green/Blue
Sky Blue x Olive Green =	100% Dark Green/Blue
Sky Blue x Sky Blue =	100% Sky Blue
Sky Blue x Cobalt =	50% Sky Blue
	50% Cobalt
Sky Blue x Mauve =	100% Cobalt
Sky Blue x Light Yellow =	100% Light Green/White
Sky Blue x Dark Yellow =	50% Light Green/White
	50% Dark Green/White
Sky Blue x Olive Yellow =	100% Dark Green/White
Sky Blue x Olive Green/Blue =	50% Cobalt
	50% Dark Green/Blue
Sky Blue x Cobalt/White =	25% Sky Blue
	25% Sky Blue/White
	25% Cobalt
	25% Cobalt/White

A Skyblue cock, a good example of the type of bird which has been winning during the recent years in England. The constant demand for size, large skull formation and giant spots has led to a type of showbird which sits, rather than stands, on the perch. Size-demand has led to the breeding of birds which can reach the perch only by climbing the wires.

The Cobalt Blue

In 1921 both the Cobalt and the Mauve made their appearance in southern France but soon appeared independently in a number of other aviaries in Europe. The Cobalt Blue budgerigar never breeds true. This means it is a heterozygous bird. If both parents are split white, then there will be twenty-five percent Whites among the young. These Whites will be of a sky blue, cobalt blue, or mauve suffusion.

Experienced breeders do not mate Cobalt to Cobalt because this mating usually produces Sky Blues and Mauves of a poorer quality than those obtained from other matings. The Mauves often are quite patchy in color and the Sky Blues are frequently small.

A popular mating is Cobalt x Sky Blue which produces young of both colors in equal numbers. Good Cobalts may be produced in many different ways, for instance, when Dark Green/blues or Olive/blues are mated with Sky Blues, Cobalts, or Mauves. The Cobalt is actually a cross between Sky Blue and Mauve.

The cobalt color varies considerably in different individuals. A breeder specializing in Cobalt production for the show bench breeds for the deep shades and frequently crosses with Greens. Cobalt x Mauve may give very good results too, depending on the ancestry of these birds. Like most hybrids, Cobalts are usually large birds. In mixed nests of Cobalts and Sky Blues, or Cobalts, Sky Blues, and Mauves, we find the Cobalts excelling the others in size and often in richness of color.

A few matings:

Cobalt x Light Green =	50% Light Green/Blue 50% Dark Green/Blue
Cobalt x Dark Green =	33⅓% Light Green/Blue 33⅓ Dark Green/Blue 33⅓ Olive Green/Blue
Cobalt x Olive Green =	50% Dark Green/Blue 50% Olive Green/Blue

Cobalt x Sky Blue =	50% Sky Blue 50% Cobalt
Cobalt x Cobalt =	33⅓% Sky Blue 33⅓ Cobalt 33⅓ Mauve
Cobalt x Mauve =	50% Cobalt 50% Mauve
Cobalt x Light Yellow =	50% Light Green/White 50% Dark Green/White
Cobalt x Olive Yellow =	50% Dark Green/White 50% Green/White
Cobalt x White Blue =	50% Sky Blue/White 50% Cobalt/White
Cobalt x Light Green/Blue =	25% Sky Blue 25% Cobalt 25% Light Green/Blue 25% Dark Green/Blue
Cobalt x Olive Green/Blue =	25% Cobalt 25% Mauve 25% Dark Green/Blue 25% Olive Green/Blue
Cobalt x Light Green/Yellow =	25% Light Green/Blue 25% Light Green/White 25% Dark Green/Blue 25% Dark Green/White
Cobalt x Sky Blue/White =	25% Sky Blue 25% Sky Blue/White 25% Cobalt 25% Cobalt/White
Cobalt x Light Yellow/White =	25% Light Green/White 25% Dark Green/White 25% Sky Blue/White 25% Cobalt/White
Cobalt x Olive Yellow/White =	25% Dark Green/White 25% Olive Green/White 25% Cobalt/White 25% Mauve/White

The Mauve

This shade is grayish and not as popular as the brilliant Blues, but is of great value to the color breeder. Large commercial breeders are willing to pay as much, or more, for one good Mauve as for two dozen budgerigars of common stock. Well-bred Mauves can do a great deal of good in a flock of indifferent birds with faded color. The best mating for production of good Mauves is the breeding of Mauve to Mauve. In other words, they should be purebred and not split to White Mauve. Split Mauve are frequently patchy in color and this must be avoided. When outcrosses become necessary, use any of the Green/blues.

A few matings:

Mauve x Light Green =	100% Dark Green/Blue
Mauve x Dark Green =	50% Dark Green/Blue 50% Olive Green/Blue
Mauve x Olive Green =	100% Olive Green/Blue
Mauve x Sky Blue =	100% Cobalt
Mauve x Cobalt =	50% Cobalt 50% Mauve
Mauve x Mauve =	100% Mauve
Mauve x Light Yellow =	100% Dark Green/White
Mauve x Dark Yellow =	50% Dark Green/White 50% Olive Green/White
Mauve x Olive Yellow =	100% Olive Green/White
Mauve x Olive Green/Blue =	50% Olive Green/Blue 50% Mauve
Mauve x Light Green/Yellow =	50% Dark Green/White 50% Dark Green/Blue
Mauve x Dark Green/Yellow =	25% Dark Green/White 25% Olive Green/White 25% Dark Green/Blue 25% Olive Green/Blue
Mauve x Mauve/White =	50% Mauve 50% Mauve/White
Mauve x Dark Yellow/White =	25% Dark Green/White 25% Olive Green/White 25% Cobalt/White 25% Mauve/White

The White Blue Series

This beautiful and well-known variety is not clearly defined in the Standard. The breast is not white, but suffused with sky blue (White Blue), or with cobalt (White Cobalt), or with mauve (White Mauve). This variety has gray wing markings of varying depth of color.

After 1920 these delicately colored birds appeared in various aviaries all over Europe. They came from blue parents, and breeders who possessed such a pair have never forgotten the thrill they experienced when the first White Blue budgerigar emerged from a nest box.

Pure Whites with black eyes, but no color suffusion and no wing markings, have not been bred from birds of the white blue series, but from Black-eyed clear Pieds.

Crossing Sky Blues, Cobalt Blues, and Mauves with White Cobalts or White Mauves frequently brings surprising results to the beginner. If a White Mauve is mated to a Cobalt, the White Mauve will breed like a true Mauve when paired to a darker color and will not produce all Cobalt/white mauves.

White Mauve x Cobalt =	50% Mauve/White Mauve 50% Cobalt/White Cobalt
White Cobalt x Cobalt =	25% Sky Blue/White Blue 25% Mauve/White Mauve 50% Cobalt/White Cobalt
White Cobalt x White Cobalt =	25% White Sky Blue 25% White Mauve 50% White Cobalt
White Cobalt x White Cobalt =	50% White Mauve 50% White Cobalt

It is necessary to watch the suffusion, whether blue, cobalt, or mauve, because all white birds of the blue series do not breed alike. They breed according to the color of their suffusion.

The Graywing Green

These varieties were known in Europe as early as 1923 and were offered for sale soon after that. In this country they were slow in appearing. California offered the Graywing Light Greens under the name "Applegreens." They are of a shade between the Light Green and the Yellow. Similarly, the Graywing Dark Green is of a shade between the Dark Green and the Yellow; and the Graywing Olive Green is between the Olive Green and the Yellow.

All Graywing varieties vary greatly in depth of suffusion and wing markings. They should be kept on a medium line, that is, birds of too light a shade, as well as those of too deep a shade, either should not be used for breeding or should be crossed with a deeper or lighter shade respectively. The young, however, will not always show an intermediate color but will often take after one or the other parent.

While the Graywing Light Green or Applegreen has become a well-known color by now, the Graywing Dark Green and the Graywing Olive are still scarce (at the present writing) and offer an ambitious show bird breeder a good opportunity to gain recognition in shows by benching good specimens of these varieties. For this purpose some experimentation with crossing the Graywing Light Greens with Dark Greens and Olives would be necessary. Breeding the Dark Green/graywing and Olive/graywing back to the parent Graywing Light Green will produce some young of the darker graywing shades. The Graywing Olive is called "Jade."

The following are a few matings:

Graywing Light Green x Olive =   100% Dark Green/Graywing

Olive/Graywing x Graywing Light Green=
                                    50% Graywing Dark Green
                                    50% Dark Green/Graywing

Graywing Dark Green x Olive/Graywing

> 25% Graywing Dark Green
> 25% Dark Green/Graywing
> 25% Graywing Olive
> 25% Olive/Graywing

In the last mating listed, half the young will be Graywings of the two dark shades, the other half will be normal looking Dark Greens and Olives, but they will carry the graywing factor in the hidden form. All Graywing Greens may be split yellow, blue or white, but there are no Graywing Yellows or Graywing Whites.

The Graywing Blue

There are three kinds of Graywings in the blue series: those with a sky blue suffusion on the breast and rump, those with a cobalt blue suffusion and those with a mauve suffusion. The rules are the same as those governing Graywing Green breeding.

While the Graywing Dark Green and Graywing Olive are very scarce, the Graywing Cobalt and Graywing Mauve have long since been developed. All the show bird breeder needs to do is perfect these varieties.

The wing markings of the Graywings should be broad. This is the outstanding feature of the Graywings and adds greatly to their attractive appearance. Interesting combinations may be worked out, such as Graywings of deeply colored suffusion on the breast with light wing markings, and Graywings with faint color on the breast and heavy wing markings. No Graywing should be allowed to become as heavily marked as the Normal. For show purposes both body color and depth of wing markings must be kept on a medium line.

The Cinnamon

The first Cinnamon appeared in England as a mutation in 1931. Its sex-linked inheritance has been fully discussed in the chapter on Genetics. Today we have

Cinnamons in all colors. They should not be confused with the common Graywing varieties. The warm brownish wing markings of true Cinnamons are somewhat different from those of the Graywing. The shaft of the long tail and flight feathers is of a distinct brownish shade, the color on the breast is softer, and the bird has a fine, silky feather texture.

At birth baby Cinnamons have reddish eyes. When comparing a newly hatched Cinnamon with a newly hatched budgerigar of one of the normal colors, the difference in eye color is very noticeable. The skin covering the eye of the young Cinnamon appears pale, while that of the normal baby is almost black. When the eyes of a baby Cinnamon open, they are distinctly reddish, gradually turning darker as the bird grows, until after

A Cinnamon hen (left) and a Lutino cock.

about two weeks the eyes appear like those of normal birds. However, they often later show a reddish glint if the light strikes them.

Cinnamons of all shades are extremely popular with breeders experimenting with new colors. The Cinnamon Cobalt shows a warm violet shade. The Cinnamon White, if bred from birds of faint suffusion, is almost pure white with black eyes. The Cinnamon Olive is of a rich golden shade quite unlike any other color. The Cinnamon Fallow and Cinnamon Opaline may be produced in all shades. Yellow Face Cinnamons of the blue series have been bred. The Cinnamon Graywings are of a lighter shade than blue and green Cinnamons and very delicate in appearance.

The Fallow
Fallows have red eyes and first appeared in 1932. They are known in all colors, but are lighter in shade than normal colors. Pure white Fallows have been bred; they look like Albinos. Fallows breed like our normal colors (N.S.L.). Fallow x Normal will give us all Normal/fallow young; they have dark eyes. For further breeding guide see page 149 and substitute Fallow for Harlequin.

Fallow Yellows are striking looking birds, pink- or ruby-eyed, and are often clear yellow with no markings whatsoever. They are larger and heavier than pure Fallow Whites, at least at the present time. Some breeders are trying to improve the stamina of the Fallow White by crossing with our normal colors.

Purebred N.S.L. Fallows have Cinnamon wing markings, even if never crossed with Cinnamon. The black pigment is missing, leaving the brown. They can easily be distinguished from Cinnamons by their eye color which is pink, while the eyes of adult Cinnamons are black. Fallow Dark Greens and Fallow Olives are birds of exceptional beauty with ruby eyes, rich brown wing markings, and golden orange breasts as described by C.H. Rogers.

The white Fallows often have faint brown wing markings, but the most valuable birds are pure white Fallows with no trace of wing markings. When purchasing a pure white bird with pink eyes, the breeder should ask for the pedigree in order to know whether or not the bird is sex-linked, whether it is an Albino or a Fallow and from what colors it was bred.

Fascinating new color combinations can be achieved by crossing Fallows with other varieties; for instance, the Yellow Face—Fallow—Opaline has been bred.

The Albino

These birds are pure white with pink eyes. Most of them have a sex-linked inheritance (S.L.), though some N.S.L. Albinos have been reported. They may be classed with the clear Fallow Whites in bird shows. Our sex-linked Albinos breed like Cinnamons (see preceding chapter under Sex Linkage). In order to breed Albinos successfully the breeder should know their ancestry. There are Albino Mauves, Albino Cobalts, Albino Blues, etc. All look alike (pure white), but breed according to their color inheritance which is masked in this species. For instance, an Albino Sky Blue hen crossed with a Mauve cock will give us nothing but Cobalt young. This shows that the invisible Sky Blue of the Albino has combined with the Mauve, giving us the intermediate shade of Cobalt. The cocks of these Cobalts will be split albino.

Albinos sometimes do not have good feather structure. The plumage looks rough and lacks luster. A cross with the silky feathered Cinnamons will greatly improve the Albino's coat of feathers. Albino hens are usually more plentiful than Albino cocks. If an Albino White Sky Blue hen is mated to a Cinnamon White Sky Blue cock, the young will be Cinnamon White Sky Blue hens and White Sky Blue/albino cinnamon cocks according to my breeding records. However, other matings have not always produced cocks split to two sex-linked varieties. Often the cocks are only split to one. It is inadvisable to cross-breed three S.L. varieties because endless test-matings would be necessary to know which cocks are split to what.

White Fallow cock crossed with Albino hen will produce black-eyed, normal colored young. In the S.L. Albino the genes for red eyes and feathers without pigment are situated in a sex chromosome, while in the White Fallow they are in the normal chromosomes. The genes responsible for red eyes and lack of pigmentation in the feathers will combine with normal genes and, therefore, will produce normally colored young. Some Albinos in adult feather show a very faint tint of color on breast and rump. This can be eliminated by crossing with Australian Gray.

The Lutino

A most striking looking yellow budgerigar is the Lutino. It is a red-eyed bird of rich, pure color without any markings. At times the eyes are dark ruby and look black. Some Lutinos are outstanding birds as regards type, size and color. The long wing and tail feathers are white. This variety is bred in the sex-linked and non-sex-linked forms. The S.L. form breeds like the Cinnamons described in the previous chapter. The N.S.L. form breeds like our normal colors. Lutinos are best mated to Dark Greens to preserve depth of color. Lutino x Lutino matings should be avoided, but split Lutino males may be used with Lutino hens. Neither Albinos nor Lutinos were produced until 1936.

It has occasionally happened that when two Lutinos or one Lutino and one Albino were mated, some of the young were normal green birds. It seems, therefore, that there are different mutations about, both looking the same and both sex-linked. The normal young cocks should be split to Lutino or also to White and Albino.

The Opaline

These unusual-looking birds are becoming extremely popular. The vivid suffusion of body color over back and wings gives them a lustrous appearance. They originated in Australia in 1932 and slightly later appeared in Europe as independent mutations. They are now widely bred in all budgie loving countries. In the United States they are increasing in number every year. They are of a sex-linked inheritance like the Cinnamon and may be bred the same way. They are bred in all the known colors. Opaline Light Greens, Opaline Dark Greens, Opaline Olive Greens, Opaline Sky Blues, Opaline Cobalts, and Opaline Golden Faced Cobalts are all very handsome birds. Opaline Yellows and Whites are not as striking looking as the other shades named. They hardly can be distinguished from the normal Yellows and Whites, but are valuable to the breeder for crossing with deeper colored varieties and Fallows.

The Opaline is a recessive to our normal colors. A normal cock paired with an opaline hen will produce Normal/opaline cocks and normal hens. For further breeding guide see chapter II, Sex Linkage. Opalines may be crossed with Cinnamons and eventually Opaline Cinnamons may be produced in the way mentioned in connection with Albino x Cinnamon matings. Young hens will be the first to show both Cinnamon and Opaline in their outward appearance. Opaline Brownwings are easier to breed, because the Brownwing factor is not sex-linked and only one sex linkage is involved.

Opalines crossed with Graywings are attractive but, as is the case in Opaline Cinnamons, they are rather pale in color. It is better to cross them with Whitewings or Yellow-wings. Extremely handsome birds are Yellow Faced Opaline Blues and Cobalts. Two black-headed Opaline Cobalts were bred in Norway, but were lost in World War II.

Opalines vary greatly in quality. In some the barring on the back of the neck is too heavy. The "V" formed by a line drawn between the wing butts and the

142

triangle between the wings on the back should be as clear of barring as possible. The best Opalines in many cases are obtained from mating an Opaline to a Normal or split Opaline. In a mixed nest Opalines can be distinguished from Normals when about ten days old by their white down. Green and blue Normals have gray down.

The Standard demands a clear "V" (mantle) combined with normal wing markings and good spots. Many breeders consider faint wing markings most attractive in Opalines and are breeding for "self colored" birds in which breast color is deep with a suffusion on faintly marked wings. These are Opaline Clearwings.

A new Opaline variety has been developed which has very little black on the wings except for a V mark of dark feathers. These are V wings. This variety crossed with Whiteflighted and Yellow Face gives us the "Splendid Opalines"—the newest and rarest and most beautiful of all Opalines. The Whiteflighted factor dilutes the dark pigment about the head and these birds instead of being yellow faced are yellow headed.

Clearwings

The collective term Clearwing has become established among breeders for the Whitewing and the Yellow-wing, though it is not quite correct. The wings are not clear, markings are visible.

Whitewings and Yellow-wings should not be confused with the normal Whites and Yellows with faint wing markings. A true Whitewing is a bird of a deep sky blue, cobalt, or mauve body color (almost as deep as that of the Normal) with faint markings on white wings. A true Yellow-wing is a bird of almost normal light, dark, or olive green body color with faint markings on yellow wings. These birds belong to the rare varieties but are bred now in this country. They are exceptionally beautiful, especially the Cobalt Whitewings and Dark Green Yellow-wings. Their body color is deeper than that of the Graywings and their wings are lighter; they form a striking contrast. Normal Blues and Greens may be split clearwing and Clearwings may be split to white or yellow. Wing markings should not be allowed to become as heavy as those of Graywings.

The Violet

This N.S.L. variety has become known only within the last decade. The true visible Violet is a Cobalt with the violet color added. These are the exhibition Violets and have a beautiful brilliant coloring, often with a pinkish sheen. Although the Violet has been called dominant, possessing two factors (V and VV), breeding experiments have shown that there is no complete dominance and more than two factors are involved. This is plainly demonstrated by the fact that we obtain various intensities in their coat of feathers. The visible Violet may have a poor violet color grading up to the deep, brilliant, pinkish Violet of the best specimens. A large number of carefully planned test matings by a trained geneticist may reveal that we are dealing with the multiple-factor hypothesis for the inheritance of quantitative characters. This does not help the practical breeder. The experience of noted Violet breeders is summarized as follows:

The **Sky Blue Violet** may have just a little violet superimposed on the sky blue, showing as a cobalt wash over the bird, more noticeable on the rump and lower breast. The last short feathers on the rump, those lying above the tail, should show a distinct violet-pinkish color.

The **Mauve Violet** is difficult to distinguish from an ordinary Mauve. Experts say each Mauve from Violet breeding should be test-mated. Some Mauve Violets throw a very good proportion of visible Violets of deep color when mated to normal Sky Blue. Mauve Violets

This bird has a beautifully straight back—an 'exhibitor's' stance. But he is 'weak upstairs' and needs mating to a hen with a huge head and 'bull' neck. This cock comes from a line of birds that all stand erect and motionless; the owner dare not allow any of them to fatten, as they all develop a roll across the shoulders. This strain has been bred, unbroken by any outside blood, for 28 years, and all possess the same characteristics.

are valuable for Violet breeding because they add a dark factor.

The **Violet carrier** is a bird with the violet coloring visible in the short feathers above the tail and sometimes a bit of violet shading about the neck and under the wings. Such a bird carries only a small amount of violet and should be bred back to Violet.

The **Violet-bred** bird is normal looking with no violet showing but of Violet parentage. It has been found to be better for breeding to Violet than a completely normal Cobalt with no Violet ancestors. Test mating is necessary.

In order to produce the handsome **visible Violets**, the breeder should choose matings producing Cobalts, as Sky Blue x Mauve = one hundred percent Cobalt, or Cobalt x Sky Blue = fifty percent Cobalt, fifty percent Sky Blue. One of the parents must be a Violet. Definite percentages of Violets and Normals in a nest cannot be given at this time because of the complexity of violet inheritance. Experienced Violet breeders rarely mate two Violets with each other. Outcrossing to good Normals improves the strain and maintains the size. The presence of a factor for "dark" must always be kept in mind. Breeders have crossed Violet with Dark Green, Olive, or dark Gray and some muddy-looking specimens were produced. These bred back to Violet or Cobalt yielded a number of beautiful deeply colored birds of rich violet coloring.

Violets have been crossed with Cinnamons, Whitewings, and Whiteflighted but sometimes, if the violet color is not strong enough, it is difficult to distinguish Violets from non-Violets in the breeds which tend to dilute body color. Violet Opalines are most desirable, however, because a deep, distinct violet color has been produced among these and they are striking looking birds.

Deeply colored normal Cobalts have at times a slight violet sheen but it is not of the typical pinkish, true violet color. For the breeding of true Violets it is necessary to obtain a real Violet which is an independent mutation and cannot be bred from normal Cobalts.

The Pieds

"Pied" means spotted; therefore, any bird which shows blotches in his feather pigmentation is a Pied. The group is sub-divided into five different varieties: 1. White and Yellowflighted collectively called Clearflighted (also called Dutch Pieds), 2. Harlequins (also called Danish Pieds), 3. Finnish Pieds, 4. Black-eyed Clear Yellows and Black-eyed Clear Whites, 5. Blackwings. All Pieds are judged as to type, size, posture, and pleasing and symmetrical color pattern. The Clears can be standardized to have black eyes and a pure yellow or pure white coat of feathers with no suffusion.

1. White and Yellowflighted are a most handsome variety and were first bred in Belgium in 1940. The black primary flight feathers are replaced by white ones in the Blues and by light yellow ones in the Greens. A light patch of varying size is seen at the back of the head, more noticeable in the Normals. Some specimens have clear flights but no patch. The tail is either white or yellow or it is dark as in the Normals. Often one tail feather is white, the other dark. It depends which one lies on top whether the tail will look light or dark.

Among the clearflighted Opalines we have some outstanding specimens with almost self-colored wings with a V mark of dark coverts edging the clear mantle (V wings). These short, dark feathers give a scalloped effect. The breast color should be kept as dark as possible. The less pigment in the feathers, the paler will be the blue color of the adult cock's cere. Mature hens of all Pied varieties develop a deep brown cere.

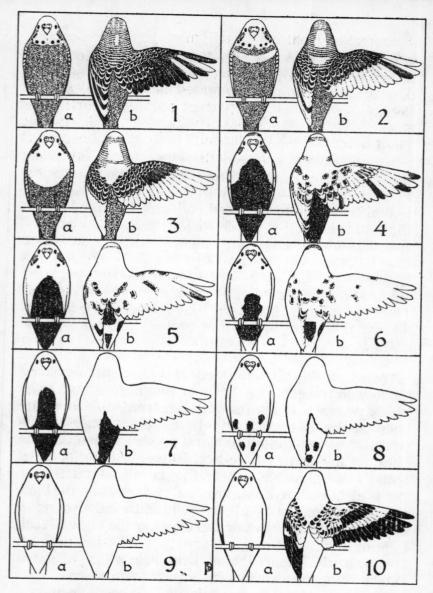

1 to 3 Whiteflighted. 1. Small patch on back of head, only two white flight feathers. 2. Ringneck. 3. Also called variegated. 4 to 6. Harlequins with diminishing pigmentation; lower breast and rump color deeper. 7 and 8. Finnish Pieds. 9. All pigment has faded out and we have the Black-eyed Clears. 10. The Blackwings with jet black markings and clear bodies, a striking contrast.

Ringnecked Opaline Clearflighted have been produced.

The Clearflighted do not breed like our Normals. Their inheritance is complicated and certainly can not be called dominant. A perfect pair of Clearflighted may throw as much as fifty percent dark flighted birds. When bred to Normal, there may be perfect Clearflighted, but most will show only a few clear primaries on one or both wings. Such birds are not symmetrically marked and should be bred back to Clearflighted or better still to the Black-eyed Clears (4) and a good proportion of perfectly marked birds will be obtained. And then there will be normal birds which may or may not carry some Clearflighted blood. Some such Normals have thrown Clearflighted when mated to Normal, but it is best to have at least a patch on the back of the head show that Pied blood is present. In fact it seems variegated birds quite frequently appear in a stud of Harlequins. The genetics of Pied breeding has been found very complex by scientists working in this field. They tell us that the apparent genetic simplicity of pied inheritance is a snare and a delusion and that some modifying genes may change a dominant to an incompletely dominant and that the absence of these modifiers will produce the recessive. As is the case with other Rares among budgies, geneticists have not yet run properly conducted experiments on their inheritance. And if they had, the results would be as involved as with those animals which are being worked on at present by specialists. Breeders in the meantime greatly enjoy the surprises the beautiful Pieds bring them. They are urged to publish breeding results from individual nests.

2. **Harlequins** are striking looking birds with the color of their bib extending about half way down their breast and with more or less dense markings on the wings, some with only polka dots. The back of the head and the mantle is clear, but a strip of black zebra

markings remains on top of the head in the adult bird. These are hooded budgerigars. The lower breast and rump should be of deep blue or green color, the darker the better. This variety is non-sex-linked and should not be crossed with sex-linked birds or the contrast between upper and lower breast will be diminished. If pure bred, Harlequins are recessive to the darker varieties and dominant to Black-eyed Clear Yellows and Black-eyed Clear Whites. Some Harlequins have been crossbred with Clearflighted (1) and as a consequence will follow the irregular pattern of Clearflighted inheritance (See preceding paragraph).

Since most Harlequins, as well as Finnish Pieds, are recessive to Normals, the following table gives the theoretical expectations. Slight variations, however, will be encountered since the amount of pigmentation in the parents varies. A normal split harlequin mated to a heavily pigmented Harlequin may produce fewer Harlequins than a Normal split Finnish Pied mated to a lightly pigmented Harlequin. A factor for split Black-eyed Clear in one of the parents will play a role.

When breeding the new rare shades, we cannot, as a rule, apply rigid percentages. More variations are encountered in the genes of the Rares (modifiers, diluters) than we find while breeding Normals. But this table will provide a general guide.

1. Harlequin x Harlequin = 100% Harlequin
2. Normal/harlequin x Normal/harlequin =
     25% Normal
     50% Normal/harlequin
     25% Harlequin
3. Harlequin x Normal/harlequin = 50% Harlequin
     50% Normal/harlequin
4. Normal/harlequin x Normal = 50% Normal
     50% Normal/harlequin
5. Harlequin x Normal = 100% Normal/harlequin

Matings 2 and 4 are not recommended because all

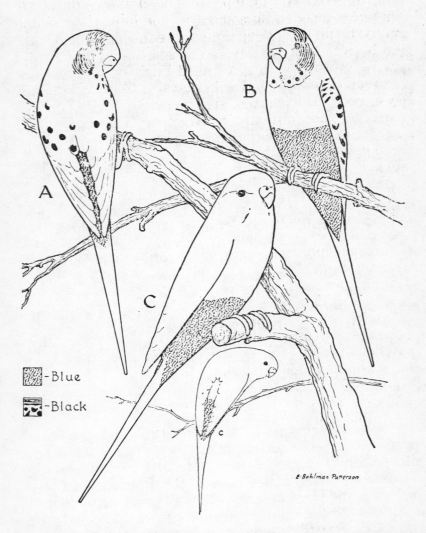

- Blue
- Black

E·Bohlman Patterson

A and **B.** Harlequins, snow white with black eyes, black markings on wings, lower breast deep blue. Harlequins are also bred in yellow with lower breast green. **C.** Finnish Pied, snow white with black eyes, head and wings completely clear, lower breast and rump deep blue. Finnish Pieds are recessive. They are an intermediate form between the Harlequin and Black-eyed Clear.

birds have to be test-mated in order to determine which carry the Harlequin factor and which do not.

3. **Finnish Pieds** are a form of Harlequin with diminished pigmentation. Finnish Pied may be substituted for Harlequin, Clearwing for Normal, in the above list. The best Finnish Pieds are pure white with no black markings on head or wings, the blue color being confined to an area about the legs and lower rump ("blue pants"). Some specimens carry ghost markings on head and wings. Crossing with Opaline Clearwings will help to eliminate these markings, but it is best to breed out the dark markings by selection rather than by crossing with Opalines because this cross will diminish the depth of blue color about the legs. We find a cross with normal Clearwings most desirable. Pure yellow Finnish Pieds with dark green "pants" are also being bred. The term "Finnish Pied" was coined by Cyril H. Rogers and E.W. Brooks of England, but word received from Europe recently indicates that these birds were first bred in Denmark, not Finland. Discussions on their genetic make-up with the first breeders of this variety, C. af Enehjelm of Finland and L. Raymaekers of Belgium, are under way and will result in a more appropriate name in the near future.

4. **Black-eyed Clear Pieds** are probably the most precious varieties among budgerigars today. They are clear with no pigmentation left but that of the large black eyes and, in the case of the Black-eyed Clear Yellows, the pure golden yellow color of their coat of feathers. Not a black, blue, or green mark is to be seen. The cere of the cock does not acquire a blue color but remains as pale as that of the Harlequin and pink-eyed Lutino or Albino. Pink- and Black-eyed are separate varieties and should not be interbred.

A clear white bird with black eyes should not be called "Black-eyed Albino" because the term "Albino" means no pigment. Black pigment is present in the eyes. Recently the term Black-eyed Lutino has been changed to Black-eyed Clear Yellow.

What makes these Black-eyed Clears so precious is the fact that by adding pigment through mating to Normals, some perfect specimens of the Pied varieties (Clearflights, Harlequins) can be produced in the first generation. Imperfectly marked Clearflights, those with only an occasional white or yellow flight feather, should be mated to a Black-eyed Clear and a good proportion of perfect specimens will be produced among the young. Black-eyed are non-sex-linked but may be crossed with a sex-linked variety such as Opaline and the cocks will then be split Opaline. The clear coat of feathers masks several varieties of Pieds which will come out when mated to pigmented birds. Black-eyed Clear Yellows may be split to clear Black-eyed Whites. A Harlequin may be split to Black-eyed Clear. Such a bird when mated to a Clear will throw fifty percent Harlequin/black-eyed clear and fifty percent Black-eyed Clear. It seems that all normal looking birds which had one clear Black-eyed for a parent will carry Pied blood. Pied inheritance has been worked out in detail by geneticists in small laboratory animals.

5. **Blackwings.** This relatively new variety should be pure white with jet black wing markings on a white ground and jet black flight feathers. Normal Greens and Blues have an off-black or brownish black color on the wings. The coal black of this striking looking bird is similar to that found in the Australian Gray, except that the wing markings are not as dense but more like those of the V wings. The feather shafts are jet black.

At the time of this writing there are a few perfect specimens in the country with breasts and rumps pure white. Many specimens, however, have irregular blue blotches on white ground.

The same variety has been bred in clear yellow with black wings; birds of this type belong to the Pied family.

Pied Matings

The following are a few actual breeding results from our records of individual pairs of the Pied family.

Perfect Whiteflighted Opaline cock x Opaline hen =
6 normal looking Opalines
2 perfect Whiteflighted
2 partially Whiteflighted

The normal looking birds have entirely clear mantles. Some have V wings. All are Opalines.

Yellowflighted Opaline Green cock x Yellowflighted Opaline Green hen, both V wings =
3 normal looking Opalines
4 perfect Yellowflighted V wing Opalines
2 partially Yellowflighted

Darkflighted Opaline cock (from Whiteflighted) x Darkflighted Opaline hen (from Whiteflighted) =
5 Darkflighted
1 partially Whiteflighted
1 Whiteflighted

The parents had a small white patch on the back of the head. If no patch shows, usually only normal young will be produced.

Harlequin cock x Normal/harlequin hen (from Harlequin x Normal) =
6 Normal/harlequin
4 Harlequins with heavily marked wings

Finnish Pied Cobalt cock x Dark Green Harlequin hen (from Black-eyed Clear) =
2 Finnish Pieds
5 Harlequins

Cobalt Whitewing/Finnish Pied cock x Finnish Pied hen =
4 Whitewing/Finnish Pied
1 Graywing/Finnish Pied
3 Finnish Pieds

The breeding results of Finnish Pieds show that the

hens have faint gray markings on the wings while the cocks are clear.

Finnish Pied cock (Blue Pants) x Normal Blue hen (daughter of Black-eyed Clear) =

4 Normals
5 Harlequins
1 Normal with white patch on back of head

Black-eyed Clear/opaline cock x Opaline Blue Hen =

7 normal looking young
5 perfect Yellowflighted
3 partially Yellowflighted
1 almost perfect Yellowflighted
1 mixture of Yellowflighted and Harlequin

The last bird looks patchy and the expression "variegated" is used for it. It proved to be an excellent breeder for Black-eyed Lutino production. The perfect Yellowflighted of this mating were Opaline V wing cocks.

Black-eyed Clear/opaline cock x Light Green Opaline hen with 2 yellow flight feathers on each wing (father to daughter mating) =

2 Normals
1 perfect Yellowflighted
1 partially Yellowflighted
4 Black-eyed Clear Yellows

"Variegated" Harlequin—Yellowflighted mixture/white cock x Harlequin Blue hen (from Black-eyed clear White) =

1 Normal
2 Whiteflighted
2 Harlequins
1 Black-eyed Clear Yellow
2 Black-eyed Clear Whites

The mating of Black-eyed Clear x Black-eyed Clear is not recommended; nor is it wise to mate a Clear to a Finnish Pied or other very weakly pigmented Pied.

The Yellow Face Blue.

The striking mutation producing a yellow face on a blue budgerigar is a comparatively recent one. A blue or cobalt breast and a golden face is a most attractive combination of color effects.

There are two main types of Yellow Faces (Y.F.), both are N.S.L. Type I has a rather faint yellow on the mask and a blue breast. There may be slight overlay of yellow on the upper part of the breast, under the bib.

Type II has a deep golden color on the face. In their nest feathers these birds have blue breasts, but in adult feathers a strong yellow overlay develops on the blue of the breast, giving it a green color. In good light an adult Y.F. Type II bird can be distinguished from a normal Green but, especially in Y.F. Type II Opalines and Cinnamons, this is often difficult. When examining the inside of an open wing of a Normal Blue, a white strip will be noticed extending across both primary and secondary flight feathers. The same is found in Type I Y.F. In Type II Y.F., however, the strip on the secondaries is yellow while that on the parimaries remains a dull white. The white area on the under tail feathers of the Normal is yellow in the Yellow Faces. Type II in addition shows yellow on the wings.

Type III Y.F. is the most beautiful of all. It is an intermediate type between Type I and Type II. The mask is of a rich golden color while the breast color remains blue. In some specimens the deep yellow color of the mask produces a yellow wash over the whole bird. The intensity of this wash varies. It may be stronger on the breast and diminish toward the legs. Some of these are called "Rainbows." Most breeders are of the opinion that Y.F. Opaline Cobalt Whitewings or Y.F. Opaline Bronzewings should be called Rainbows, provided the Y.F. factor produces the right shading. Sometimes it is more or less evenly distributed and the whole bird appears to have a yellowish green shade. These are Sea-greens and very

Inside of wing of Yellow Face Type II.
Primaries show a dull white strip.

Secondaries are yellow in Type II, dull white
in Type I and Normal.

attractive. The inside strip on the flight feathers remains a dull white in some birds but carries a varying amount of yellow in others.

It has been stated in bird publications that Y.F. is dominant over Normal and that these birds may carry one or two factors for Y.F. A Y.F. double factor is supposed to produce one hundred percent single factor when mated to White-faced Normal. I have made many test matings with Y.F. from different sources but have not been able to detect a double factor, nor is the Y.F. always dominant. I have crossed Type I and Type III and received all White-faced young. The sons of this mating were mated to Normal White Blue hens and produced almost one hundred percent Y.F. young, some Type I, some Type III. This was a surprising result considering both parents were white faced. It is, however, not a uniform finding.

Hundreds of genes are involved in the production of Y.F. There are modifiers and diluters and we cannot predict expectations in percentages. Geneticists employ long formulas to account for all the possible combinations. These are too complicated and not practical for the breeder to consider. Experience in the breeding room is what counts. One to three Y.F. young may be expected in a nest from one Y.F. parent and the other parent White-faced. At times only an occasional Y.F. is received from such matings, at other times none—a disappointing result. The more Y.F. is concentrated in a strain, the better the yield will be.

Y.F. have been crossed with Opalines, Cinnamons, Brownwings, Grays, Albinos, Whiteflighted, Clearwings, Pieds, and of course, White Blues, Sky Blues, Cobalts, and Mauves. Many of the young are breathtaking in their luminous coat of feathers. This is especially true of those which are not too light in color.

The Brownwing or Bronzewing

This is one of the newest varieties and is still quite rare. Brownwings are not related to Cinnamons and cannot be bred from them. They are a non-sex-linked variety. Wing color in Brownwings varies; there are light, medium, and dark Brownwings. These are not clearly defined classes, rather a grading of brown shades. The lighter ones are called Bronzewings. The lightest of these are called "Selfs" in the Opaline series. Wing markings are almost absent and the breast color washes over the wings. They are very

158

beautiful birds. Most Brownwings are split to White or Clearwing, some to Albino, Lutino, or Clearflighted. Mating to White is not advisable because all young will be split white and eventually the brown wing color fades and the birds will look like Graywings.

Too much crossbreeding is done of the rare colors. A breeder of Brownwings should endeavor to develop a pure strain of normal or Opaline Brownwings. This is best done by mating Brownwing to Brownwing or the brown or bronzewing factor may be scattered and lost. There are a number of breeders who say the most perfect "Rainbows" are found among the Y.F. Bronzewings in blue or cobalt. The Y.F. factor has to be of the right intensity to produce the Rainbow shading.

Yellow Face Opaline Blue or Cobalt Brownwings are a most handsome variety, usually strong and good sized-birds with a deeper body color than Opaline Cinnamons. It is necessary to obtain a reliable pedigree because Opaline Cinnamons have been sold for Opaline Brownwings and vice versa. These two varieties should not be interbred. Some specimens do not develop the full brown wing color until the second year of life.

The Crested

Two main types of crests on top of the head are recognized, the canary crest and the cockatiel crest. Both crests occasionally are found on one bird. The crests are usually small, often just a ruffle of feathers, sometimes "bangs" or various other feather arrangements of different sizes have appeared. Robert Centofanti reports that Crested bred to Normal at times does not produce any crested birds. However, one of these "crest-bred" young bred back to its crested parent will produce some crested young.

It seems the variety is a semi-dominant. Crested have been bred to Crested with no bald spots resulting as has been observed in canaries. According to B.H.S.

Genders there seems to be a lethal factor when Crested is bred to Crested; not all young grow up. All in all, the percentage of Crested produced by the various matings is low which makes good Crested birds quite valuable. No uniform results as to their genetic make-up have so far been published.

The Australian Gray

This new variety is gaining rapidly in popularity. The pure pearl gray color of the lighter shades is so attractive that these birds are well-liked as pets in spite of the fact that the pet-loving public usually is partial to color, principally blue. In purebred Australian Grays (and also in Gray/whites) the cheek patches are gray. The tail and long flight feathers are jet black, while in our dark Normals the tails are dark blue. Roughly, there are three intensities of the gray body color: light, medium, and dark. There are normal and opaline Grays, both usually large and well spotted.

When mated to normal Blue or Green, either all young will be gray or the gray color will merge with the blue or green and give us Gray Blue or Gray Green. The cheek patches will be of a brilliant French blue color quite unlike the usual purple color. Gray Whites and Gray Yellows also may be bred. This shows that the Australian Gray is not always dominant but may form a blend between Gray and the color it is mated to. Some normal Blues may be raised from Gray/white mated to Blue. There are also birds with the jet black tail feathers of the Gray, and pure blue body color. It seems the Gray should be classed with the incompletely dominant varieties. Purebred Grays will throw all Gray young. Grays are not sex-linked, both cocks and hens may be gray if one parent was gray.

Our favorites are the Gray Greens with their soft mustard body color. Gray Yellows, too, are most attractive with their deep yellow coat of feathers, which

160

may look golden. There are Cinnamon Grays with gray breasts and brown wing markings and brown tails. They are not Brownwings according to our test matings.

Grays are used for Albino breeding because an Albino masking the Australian Gray color will not show any blue suffusion. They are also used to deepen the color of Violets. The first cross may produce muddy-looking birds, but a back cross will produce some birds of outstanding deep violet color. Yellow Face Gray may be very beautiful if the Y.F. is confined to the mask and does not spread over the breast. Possibly birds with almost white breasts and black or brown wing markings may be produced by crossing with Opaline Pieds. Gray Greens have been bred in the Clearflighted form and, curiously enough, the clear flight feathers are partially white, though the bird has a yellow face from the green factor. Any green bird would be expected to be Yellowflighted. The Gray Green, therefore, combines both color varieties in the visible form. There is a recessive Gray which crops out among the birds imported from continental Europe.

Other Colors

Slates are similar but are a sex-linked variety. Budgerigars which could be called the opposite of Clearwings have been bred. They have deeply marked wings and throat spots with a very faint body color. Plum-color-eyed birds have appeared in Europe in all colors since 1932. More recent are green budgies with white faces. Budgerigars with white or yellow breasts and black wing markings have been reported. Lutinos and golden yellow pink-eyed Opalines with lacy brown wing markings are the latest of our array of new colors.

Half-siders show one color on one side of the body and another color on the other side. Half-siders with a completely blue cere are males and those with a tan cere are females and usually are fertile, but produce normal young only (somatic mutation). Half-siders with half of their cere blue, the other half tan have been reported; these birds do not breed. Half-siders are found in practically all color combinations as blue on the right side and yellow on the left side, or Cinnamon Green on the right side and Cinnamon Cobalt on the left side.

This list of colors is imcomplete. New colors spring up constantly and breeders create new effects by crossing the various shades.

The scarcity of the new varieties tempts the breeder to inbreed more than is good for the birds. It should be remembered that mutations are usually weak at first and frequent outcrossing to Normals of good type is strongly advised. The same applies to the breeding of all pink-eyed varieties. Patience will bring its reward.

IV Housing

General Considerations

We shall not describe here how an aviary should be built as we recently published a book on this matter (*Building an Aviary*). It is however difficult to give details in just one chapter since there is such a wide variety of climates in our country. In some sections birds can be kept outdoors all through the year; in others they can be kept outdoors only in summer, or rather from spring to late fall.

In all cases the prospective breeder is advised to contact other local breeders and see how they have solved the problem of housing. Joining a local bird club will supply the novice with ideas at its monthly meetings. It is advisable to gather as much information as possible, plan everything carefully, and have breeding and flight cages ready before birds are ordered. When birds are obtained first, during a spurt of enthusiasm, and then later shifted about and disturbed by carpentry work, etc., the fancier should not be surprised if the birds fail to breed. If breeding cages are placed in kitchens or living rooms with lights disturbing the birds after sunset, a few young may be raised but systematic production of good birds is impossible under such conditions.

Attics and basements have been successfully converted into bird rooms, but many attics become too warm in the summer unless very well insulated and ventilated. However, if large sky lights are cut into the roof, these will supply air and direct sunlight in the summer. All window spaces should be covered with wire netting to prevent the escape of birds when the windows are opened. Basements in houses which are heated during the winter can be made into nice bird rooms but during the summer they frequently become too damp. Many breeders keep their birds in either attic or basement in the winter and turn them into outdoor flights in the summer.

In crowded cities where outdoor flights are a luxury which the breeder has to forego, a spare room in the house or a garage can be converted into a birdroom. We have seen some double garages made into beautiful, well-equipped aviaries. A breeder may line two walls with breeding cages, a third wall with long flight cages, and have the sink and vestibule with two entrance doors occupy the fourth wall. A heating unit is placed either in the center or against the fourth wall. Temperatures should be regulated by means of a thermostat, allowing the temperature to drop at night to eight or ten degrees below the daytime level. Daytime temperatures as a rule are kept around seventy degrees Fahrenheit. During a hot spell in summer, wet towels should not be used to cool off the birds. High humidity is bad for budgerigars. Instead, plenty of fresh drinking water should be supplied.

This aviary is well insulated. Outside flights connect with the inside portion. Budgies go freely in and out.

A door should never open directly to the outside because even when kept in cages and individual flights, birds will occasionally be loose in the aviary and may easily escape when the breeder or visitors enter or leave. A vestibule with one inside and one outside door prevents such accidents. A workbench or storage space is often fitted into the vestibule. '

Ventilation is provided by transom-type windows or exhaust fans above the tiers of breeding cages or, still better, by skylights which admit sunlight when opened wide in the summer. Drafts should be guarded against very carefully. Drafts cause colds in birds, often resulting in diarrhea which in a short time saps a bird's strength.

The aviary should be well insulated to prevent excessively high temperatures in summer. It also must be rat and mouseproof. A cement covered floor should be laid flush with brick walls. A drain should be provided to taked care of the water when the aviary is washed with a hose or the birds are given an artificial rain with a spray.

The ideal aviary is the one where outside flights can be attached to the building. Flights should be built only on one side of the building, because flights on opposite sides will expose the birds inside to drafts. These outdoor flights are best when partially roofed over to protect birds from too much sun or rain. Most birds like a little rain on their feathers but should not be forced to become soaked. Part of their flights must always be shaded. Sun has not only beneficial, but also injurious qualities, and different species of birds vary in their requirement of direct sunlight. Outside flights should communicate with inside flights or shelters so the birds can go out or in at will.

Where birds have to be kept indoors in the summer, breeders are often tempted to install quartz or Vita glass windows which allow ultraviolet rays to pass through. It is useless, however, to go to this expense unless the quartz glass windows are polished once a day or oftener in sooty cities. Any thin film of dust, soot, or deposits from rain filters out the ultraviolet rays of the sun and the windows then have no advantage over ordinary window glass. All wire netting (hardware cloth) must be brushed thoroughly with a stiff wire brush to remove loose particles of solder which will poison birds if eaten.

Although budgerigars, when kept entertained in spacious flights with other birds of their kind, do not do much damage to woodwork by chewing, it is safer to have the framework of flights made of metal rather than wood. The netting should be made of one-half inch hardware cloth. This is not mouseproof. Some breeders for this reason prefer one-quarter inch hardware cloth which prevents mice from entering the aviary and eating seeds. However, the birds inside cannot be seen as well through this closely woven mesh.

The minimum number of flights is three: one for the cocks, one for the hens, and one nursery flight for the young. These flights are for non-breeding birds, contain no nest boxes, and are used for resting and maturing birds, as well as for those offered for sale or kept for exhibition in bird shows. Large establishments often have more flights: one for cocks of valuable blood lines to be kept for breeding and exhibition, one for hens of the same quality, one cock and one hen flight for surplus stock, and one or more flights for immature stock. If space permits, much time is saved if birds retained for breeding are kept in separate quarters from birds to be sold.

In either case young birds should always be kept separate from mature ones because freshly weaned budgies benefit a great deal by extra feeding of a little nestling food every other day and require more oats for several months than mature birds. Old birds get too fat if fed the same amount of oats as is necessary for growing stock.

Perches may be installed in two different ways. Either natural branches or even small trees are mounted in the aviary, or regular perches (dowel rods) are arranged in such a manner that birds sitting on the upper ones cannot foul the lower. Natural tree branches are used only for the larger flights because in small ones they obstruct flight space. The bark is soon chewed off, but the bare branches serve the purpose just as well. They look attractive and give the acrobatic budgerigar more opportunity for climbing. Branches also vary in thickness which is good for the birds' feet. Budgerigars prefer twigs of small diameter to thick perches.

In smaller flights and flight cages, perches should be installed at either end with none in the middle as the purpose of flights is to give the birds flying exercise. For this reason perches are mounted close to the ceil-

In an aviary of this type all sorts of little gadgets can be fixed up for the birds' (and their owners') amusement. Even breeding is possible.

Young birds should always be kept separate from mature ones, because freshly weaned budgies benefit a great deal by extra feeding of a little nestling food every day and require more oats for several months more than mature birds. Old birds get too fat if fed the same amount of oats as is necessary for growing stock.

ing with none between the upper perches and the ground. The exercise birds get from flying up and down is important and aids in keeping them fit and slim and in good type, if such is their inheritance. Perches should be of different diameters, varying from one-quarter to three-eighths of an inch. Floors are made of cement and supplied with a drain.

The ideal flights are those equipped with running water and fountains. A cement floor with a ditch which collects the water from the fountain is not hard to install. The basin of the fountain should be shallow since budgerigars do not bathe in deep water. The fountain should be so mounted that it provides perching places for the birds where the spray reaches them. Fountain basins and ditches must be brushed out regularly with a stiff broom. Where fountains cannot be installed, a shallow bathing dish is appreciated by the birds, especially if some carrot tops, grasses, or other greens are placed over it. Budgerigars love to roll in wet greens.

Regarding the sizes of flights, it must be stated that the larger they are, the better for the birds. Crowding birds into too small quarters makes them very nervous because some of the birds constantly disturb others which want to take a nap during long summer days. This eventually impairs the health of the colony and encourages cannibalism. Minimum space for a group of nonbreeding budgerigars may be figured in the following way: all birds are chased to one end of the flight. When all have come to rest on the perches, there should be a space of at least two inches between birds. They are then crowed but when left alone, some will be on the floor or hanging to the wires. Consequently, space between them will be increased giving those birds which want to take a rest a chance to relax for a short time. This method of figuring space applies only when there are no perches in the center or halfway between top and bottom of flights. As explained before, such spaces should be left open for flight exercise.

The longer and the higher flights are, the better. When about seven feet high, three tiers of perches may be placed above each other at either end. Flight cages only three or four feet high should not have more than two tiers of perches at either end. Swings and ferris wheels should be used only in very large flights and then hung to one side.

Where space does not permit the consideration of large flights, smaller units called flight cages must do. The minimum length for a flight cage is five to six feet.

The minimum depth is two feet, but if possible, it is better to build the cage three feet feet deep because it will accommodate more birds. Minimum height is three feet, but five feet is preferable.

Flights are so constructed that the breeder can walk into them, but flight cages are not large enough for that and, therefore, wire fronts should be made removable. When repainting time comes, the breeder takes out the fronts, permitting him to reach the back wall and all the corners. Wire netting is used exclusively for large flights, but for flight cages either wire netting or straight wires one-half inch apart can be used. Birds can be seen better through wires than through netting. An attractive wire cloth is obtainable in one hundred foot rolls, spaced one-half by two inches. Wire netting may be sprayed with black enamel by means of a spray can. The black color allows a better view of the birds than unpainted netting. The flight cages generally used are of the box-type, but often one side is made of wire instead of wood, giving the birds more light and air.

Naturalistic Aviaries

Most attractive displays can be designed by equipping an aviary with natural tree trunks. Budgerigars greatly enjoy excavating their nest cavities. Holes may be drilled into an old tree trunk in the places where the owner likes to have nests and the birds will continue widening the hole and chewing a hollow inside for their eggs and young. On account of the difficulty of keeping such nests clean, it is advisable not to allow more than one nest of young to be raised in gourds and tree trunks. The gourds are then taken down, cleaned, the droppings in the hollows scooped out and cavities sprayed with a mite-killing solution. Nest boxes with the bark adhering may be hung up in other places, but all should be roofed over or rain may run into the nest cavities. A fountain may be installed and a rock garden planted outside the aviary to cover the cement foundation.

As a rule it is inadvisable to keep hook-billed birds in the same aviary with other birds, but where there is

Each breeding cage has two perches, a removable tray, and a wire screen. Homemade breeding cages like these have disadvantages (they are less easily cleaned and sanitized, for example) that make them less useful than commercial cages and breeding set-ups designed specifically for breeding budgies.

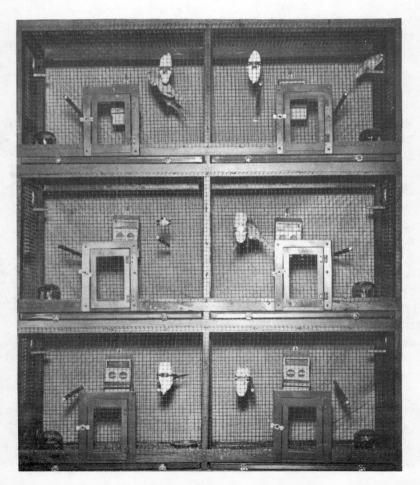

ample space with many hiding places behind shrubbery, and nooks and corners are provided by means of boards or heavy branches, an assortment of different birds can and have been kept together without harm. Any fighter among the birds, however, must be removed.

Breeding Cages
The size of breeding cages for one pair of budgies varies with the available space. They should be box-type. Here again, the larger the cage, the better. Some breeders advise breeding cages three feet long to allow for some flying space for the birds. The general experience, however, is that a cage two feet long is of sufficient size. Breeding birds do not need much exercise while busy raising young. If they feel like stretching their wings, they do this by flapping them while sitting on a perch. Only two successive nests are taken from good stock; the remainder of the year the birds get plenty of exercise in the flights. In "All-Pets Magazine's" third annual budgerigar edition W. Watmough pointed out that cage breeding in England, too, has been found not to harm the birds. A depth of one foot and a height of one and one-half feet are the minimum dimensions for breeding cages. Part of the height will be taken up by a tray and a screen above it. The screen is made of one-quarter inch hardware cloth in a metal frame and the tray of sheet metal. Both are removable for cleaning purposes. Some breeders do not favor a screen for breeding cages. In well-kept quarters, cages without screens have been used successfully.

Fronts may be made of either one-half inch wire netting or wire bars one-half inch apart. The one-half by two inch netting is becoming most popular. Doors should be in front and large enough to admit seed hoppers. A convenient size for doors is about eight inches long and five inches high.

This is quite a nice Gray cock. The beak is well tucked in and there is no hump or roll of fat across the shoulders.

Breeding cages. Note the sliding trays; they simplify cleaning operations.

Each breeding cage has two perches, although some breeders use only one, the second one being supplied by the perch of the nest box. Where long rows of breeding cages line the sides of an aviary, the nest boxes are attached to the fronts, free of the doors. If a tier of double breeding cages is placed in a sun parlor or spare room, the nest boxes are hung up at the sides. The arrangement depends on the space available and the number of birds being kept. In all cases it is necessary that the birds can see other breeding pairs. Wire partitions made of one-quarter inch hardware cloth serve this purpose, as well as admitting more air and light to box-type cages. If the partitions are removable two or more breeding cages may be converted into a flight cage.

Tiers of box-type breeding cages may be placed opposite each other or at right angles. They are made either of wood or metal. Aluminum cages do not require painting. Wooden cages are painted and enameled white inside and any color of the breeder's choice outside. It is most important that the paint and enamel are of a brand not containing lead, because the lead found in paints is extremely toxic to birds. The label analysis on each can of paint must be checked. Tiers of cages in the home may be placed either on a sturdy table, on shelves, or hung on the wall. They should not be placed directly on the floor unless supplied with legs, because budgerigars rarely breed in cages on the floor.

In large aviaries the space below the breeding cages, as well as above them under the ceiling, is used to advantage for storage space. Doors in front of storage shelves give the aviary a neat appearance.

Seed Hoppers

It is not practical to use open dishes for seeds. Hulls accumulate among the seeds and have to be blown out daily, a tedious task for the breeder. Whenever the birds flap their wings, hulls are scattered about the cages. To eliminate such annoyances, seed hoppers have drawers to catch the hulls and can be emptied. Hoppers are refilled every few days or once a week, depending on the size of the hoppers and the number of birds. Metal hoppers are superior to wooden ones.

Water Containers

There are various water receptacles on the market. Simple, open water dishes are easily cleaned and refilled daily. If placed free of perches, they will not become contaminated by droppings, but budgerigars have a habit of throwing greens, oat hulls, pieces of cuttlebone, etc. into the water if the dishes are kept on the floor. Inverted bottles may be attached to the outside of the cage.

Running water has been installed by some breeders. Each cage contains an opening of the water pipe equip-

A wooden nest box opened to show the entrance hole and the concave removable base.

ped with a dripping device and a screened funnel to catch the water.

Nest Boxes

Sizes of nest boxes vary somewhat. We like large nest boxes so the hen can push young from the first clutch out of the way when she begins to lay her second clutch of eggs. However, the boxes should not be too large. It has happened that hens have become lost in them and laid several clutches of eggs in different corners. Good overall dimensions are about eight inches wide, six inches deep, and nine or ten inches high. Some means of ventilation should be supplied at the top, either by drilling holes or nailing the top loosely to the sides.

The entrance hole for the birds measures approximately one and one-half inches in diameter. Some breeders prefer nest boxes with perches (inserted about an inch below the nest holes); others do not.

The only way to prevent mites from multiplying in nest boxes is thorough cleaning every other day when all young have hatched. Some breeders advise treating wooden boxes with a good grade of spar varnish. If mites are present, nest boxes may be sprayed from the inside with one of the advertised mite-killing solutions after removing the young. Only those boxes not in use at the moment are sprayed or only a small amount of spray is placed under removable bottoms.

Further Equipment

Every aviary should contain a heatable hospital cage or an electric heater with which heat treatments can be given to sick birds. Straight scissors, nail scissors, a pair of strong nail clippers, and a magnifying glass should always be kept on hand. Magnifying glasses are used to examine the internal organs of a dead bird, to detect the spoor of mites among the feathers of a live bird, or to get a better view of mite colonies under nest box bottoms or in other places. Mites themselves can be seen with the naked eye, but it is interesting to watch them crawl about under moderate magnification. Curious breeders often examine seeds and grit with a magnifying glass. They are obtainable in different qualities; the inexpensive ones give weaker magnification.

A high magnification for special research work can be obtained by using a pocket microscope. Although a simple magnifying glass will suffice for the bird breeder, the microcosmos revealed by a higher magnification proves fascinating to those who like to penetrate into a world ordinarily hidden from human sight. Microbes, however, cannot be seen with a pocket microscope; they have to specially prepared and stained and then placed under a regular microscope, such as is used in scientific laboratories. It takes much training to recognize microbes even then.

The contents of our medicine cabinet for birds are table salt (iodized in the Great Lakes region), Epsom salts or Glauber's salt (to be used only as an emergency treatment in case of acute poisoning), a jar of petroleum jelly, and whiskey for stimulating weakened birds.

Cod-liver oil is best kept in the refrigerator. A large container for seeds which are treated with cod-liver oil, and a spray for spraying birds with water, soap for cleaning food and water receptacles, and a soapless powder for washing birds concludes the list of principal equipment. Some breeders in addition keep a bottle of disinfectant solution on hand and those who fear mites keep a mite-killing solution with hand spray or electric steam vaporizer in the aviary.

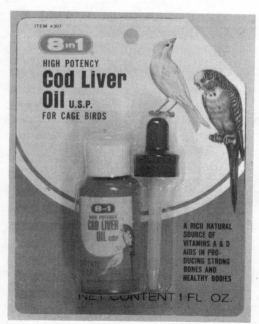

Cod-liver oil supplements designed for use with cage birds and conveniently packaged in small units to avoid spoilage are available at pet shops selling birds and supplies.

Budgies are in general very healthy and vigorous birds, and only a small percentage of them actually get sick. Still, besides having a hospital cage maintaining an even temperature night and day of 70°F., fanciers should keep some medicines and preventatives and supplements on hand.

Another object worth keeping in a large aviary is an empty seed bag in which to collect the many soft body feathers dropped by the birds. After the feathers have been cleaned by a professional, they can be made into fine down pillows. Another by-product which should not be wasted, since it serves as valuable fertilizer for potted plants or the garden, is the excrement of the birds. A scraper aids removal.

A modern and labor-saving way of cleaning large aviaries is to obtain a vacuum cleaner unit on a small truck which does away quickly with dirt scraped from the trays of breeding and flight cages. Floor and trays are then hosed and the vacuum cleaner again employed to suck up excess water. This will prevent too much moisture in the air after cleaning. Chicken farms and scientific laboratories where work on animals and birds is done on a large scale are beginning to adopt this most efficient method.

Three Breeding Record Charts

Every aviary should have stud charts which record each bird. Most breeders keep cards on the nest boxes, recording eggs and young, to which nests they were transferred, breeding behavior of the parents, etc. The information on the nest box cards is transferred to the permanent record sheets which fit an eleven by eight and one-half inch standard loose leaf notebook. They are a great time saver in locating a certain bird and determining its pedigree.

1. Breeding Record. All young of a particular pair of parents will be recorded and no mention made of transfers. A code number is assigned to each breeding pair and this number is then copied down on the nest box card. Date L.: Date laid.

Date H.: Date hatched.

2. The first column contains leg band numbers of breeders, consecutively arranged. From the Previous Breeding Code it can be seen at a glance

BREEDING RECORD

SEASON _____
CODE NO. _____

BREEDERS	COLOR	BAND NO.	PREVIOUS CODE	DATE HATCHED	REMARKS
COCK					
SIRE					
DAM					
HEN					
SIRE					
DAM					

_____ DATE MATED _____   _____ DATE RESTED _____

FIRST NEST					SECOND NEST				
DATE L	DATE H.	COLOR	SEX	BAND NO.	DATE L.	DATE H.	COLOR	SEX	BAND NO.

REMARKS   REMARKS

1953 ALL-PETS BOOKS INC.   P.O. BOX 151   FOND DU LAC, WISCONSIN, U.S.A.

2

REGISTRY AND PREVIOUS BREEDING RECORD

BAND NO.	COLOR	SEX	CODE HATCHED	PREVIOUS BREEDING CODE						

3

DISPOSITION RECORD

BAND NO.	CODE NO.	COLOR	SEX	DISPOSITION	DATE	PRICE

when and how often a particular bird was bred. Performance in the breeding room and pedigree can be looked up by noting the Code number and turning to the Breeding Record (sheet one).

3. All young are recorded in the first column by their leg band numbers, consecutively arranged. This is a great help when catching a bird out of the flight. Running one's finger down the first column, the leg band number is quickly noticed and the code number looked up in the Breeding Record (sheet one). Age and parentage of the bird is hereby determined in an instant. The code numbers in the second column will not run consecutively. Under Disposition name and address of the purchaser is recorded.

We use two loose leaf notebooks, one for the Breeding Record (one), the other for sheets two and three. It is more convenient to have one book open while leafing through the other. The sheets have holes punched at the top margin to fit standard eleven by eight and one-half inch loose leaf notebook. These holes should be enforced with stickers to prevent tearing.

Shipping Boxes

Shipping boxes are made of wood and vary in size according to the size and number of birds to be shipped. It is important that these shipping crates be so large that the birds are not crowded. A perch is mounted inside. A water container may be omitted and a piece of celery stalk or carrot substituted. The floor is covered with seeds. It is not necessary to add grit, since birds have a reserve of grit in their gizzards which lasts them a few days. The upper half of the front wall consists of wire netting or fly screen and is best built with a backward slope in order to assure the birds of a sufficient air supply, should the boxes during shipping be placed close to each other. Either the back wall is constructed with a sliding door, a top board which can be lifted off, or the front is provided with a wire screen which can be pulled off when birds are placed into or taken out of the shipping box.

It is most important that birds be protected against draft during transport. Never should there be any cross ventilation in a shipping crate. If the upper half of the front wall consists of wire netting, this will admit enough air, but during cold weather the wire must be covered with one layer of cheese cloth. It is not wise to ship in very hot weather. Of course, all breeders avoid shipping in zero weather; as a rule they do not ship during temperatures below twenty degrees Fahrenheit. Sometimes birds must be shipped at a certain date to reach a bird show in time, regardless of weather conditions. A draftproof shipping box will safeguard their health.

Shipping labels for live birds are obtainable and should be used in preference to writing "Live Birds" on the box in long hand. Large printed letters in red or black on a white label impress the many people who handle birds during transit, and loss or delay may be avoided by this means. In addition to "LIVE BIRDS" the label should show in bold type the words, "KEEP OUT OF DRAFT," "DO NOT DELAY," and "THIS SIDE UP." "LIVE BIRDS" pasted on each side and the back of the box further insures careful handling. Birds are shipped either by railway express or air express. Where there is an airport at the point of destination, air express is preferable.

V Exhibiting

Bird Shows

There is nothing more stimulating to the cage bird breeder than exhibiting the fruit of his labors in bird shows where his birds are placed side by side with those produced by other breeders and appraised by a qualified judge who is selected to award prizes to the best birds in each class. Each cage has a tag attached to it which identifies the bird as well as the owner, but the name of the owner is not visible before judging; only when all birds have been judged, and prizes awarded, may the tags be opened. It then becomes known who owns the great champion and who has won first, second, or third prizes. Ribbons, trophies, and diplomas are awarded and the excitement is great.

Most national and local shows are held in the fall of the year and birds are shipped to the larger shows from all over the country. The large the show, the keener is the competition and the greater the honor when a blue ribbon or even a rosette is earned. Breeders come from great distances to be present at these events and much "shop talk" goes on.

Bird exhibitions in this country have not yet achieved the importance which they enjoy in Europe, but with the steadily rising interest in cage birds the general public is becoming more and more aware of the attraction a display of budgerigars offers.

Each year a larger variety of colors is seen on the show bench. Judges at times have difficulty deciding whether an oddly colored bird is in the right class or not. Some may look like Cinnamons, yet they are Brownwings, quite a different variety. Then there are "Luminous," "Rainbows," and "Sea-greens." These are attractive names but do not help to classify the

Pre-exhibition Time Table

Eight weeks before show	Four weeks before show
Catch out likely candidates.	Place in individual show cages.
Pull damaged long feathers.	Eliminate those with obvious faults.
Check on cleanliness.	
If too fat, give a pinch of Epsom salts in an ounce of water with an eyedropper into the beak every three days. Stop feeding oats.	Pull spot feathers if necessary.
	Wash only those birds which are dirty. Some need only wing and tail feathers washed.
If too thin, feed plenty of oats.	Check on condition.
Place in roomy flights and keep in even temperature.	Spray twice a week.
	Gradually discontinue cod-liver oil.
	Place in clean show or training cages for short periods. Train to sit up in show position.

Two weeks before show	Three days before show.
Make selection.	Stop spraying.
Pick substitutes.	Place in show cages and train.
Spray twice a week.	Return to clean flight or training cages.
Train to sit properly in show cages every day or every other day.	Allow for plenty of sleep.
Return to flight or training cage with show cage attached.	Have all show and transport cages scrupulously clean.

bird. We have been shown about six different kinds of budgies, all called "Luminous." All were Yellow Face, some on White Blue, some on Yellow or clear White, Opaline, or Whitewing. One was an ordinary Y.F. type II, almost green. Rainbows and Sea-greens are Yellow Face Type III differing in intensity and distribution of the yellow overlay.

Birds benched for the purpose of being judged are exhibited in standard show cages, one bird to a cage although one does occasionally see a pair placed in one cage. Although open wire cages of various shapes are permissible on the show bench, the birds displayed in them are at a distinct advantage. Budgerigars will climb about the roof of the cage instead of sitting still in show position. Perches often become dislodged when light-weight wire cages are carried to the judge. Birds exhibited for sale or for display only do not need to be in special show cages, but are often shown in groups in large cages of any size and shape. Progressive breeders as well as importing houses can achieve valuable recognition by designing special flight cages for this purpose. We remember one which was equipped with tree branches on which brown oak leaves still clung. Among them a number of nests could be detected and a variety of colorful birds from many countries of the world flew about, chirping and singing happily. Another large cage was made of plastic and contained a variety of rare shades of budgerigars in plain sight through the clear plastic walls with no bars or wire netting obstructing the observer's view. Still another was a miniature naturalistic aviary with nest boxes inside made of logs with the bark attached. A densely packed group of spectators is always seen in front of such beautiful displays, fascinated by the antics and love making of the birds.

Information on how cage bird exhibitions are conducted is best obtained by joining a bird club and attending its meetings, and by visiting bird shows. Experience is the best teacher and a novice should not be timid about sending his birds to a show for fear that they may suffer by comparison to those of experienced

Opposite: This budgie hen shows typical Pied markings. She is ready for any exhibition!

breeders. It often happens that such birds win over those of the "old timers" and even if they do not win, the novice will learn where his shortcomings lie, giving him the chance to correct any faults in the birds before the shows of the following year. Most bird clubs encourage the beginner by special novice classes and the inexperienced breeder is advised to take advantage of this. After he has once been an exhibitor, the spirit of this fascinating sport will take hold of him and he will not want to miss any future shows.

Showcage training for a batch of young budgies. Cages are arranged on a mock-up of a judging bench and are continuously moved around. The birds become accustomed to the judging stick.

Preparing a Bird for Exhibition

A few general rules should be mentioned. First, the bird must be in good feather, should not show any signs of molt or have any tail or wing feathers missing, should be bright and alert and in perfect health. This is what is meant by the expression "the bird is in condition." A bird with lumps about the head, face, feet, or legs should never be sent to a bird show, because lumps are mostly due to disease of a contagious nature, and such a bird may infect other birds. Scaly feet may be caused by mite infestation, and mites too will attack other birds. Naturally, birds so afflicted have no chance to win in a bird show.

Second, the bird must be accustomed to its show cage. Training show specimens starts several weeks in advance of the fall shows. Most breeders like to attach a standard show cage to the larger cage in which the birds are kept. The birds are allowed to go freely in and out of the show cage, in this way becoming acquainted with it. Then each bird is placed in a show cage by itself and given some training in sitting up straight and quietly without dashing wildly back and forth, or crouching in corners, or doing acrobatics as budgerigars are apt to do. Excellent birds have been disqualified by the judge because they would not sit still. The "steadying process" is done with a pencil or stick with the owner's face close to the cage. Budgies which are used to the proximity of their owners do not need much training. Although a bird is not supposed to be wild, an untamed bird is the better performer on the show bench. A bird which has been petted will try to nibble at the judge's fingers and not sit up in show position.

Third, the bird must be clean. It should be sprayed with water about three times a week for two weeks preceding a show with the exception of the last few days, since spraying dulls the natural luster of the feathers. If the feathers are very soiled, they may need to be soaped. In general, breeders like to avoid this because it necessitates handling the bird and some feathers may become frayed as a consequence. If it has to be done, however, it is best to use one of the soapless powders which do not leave scum on the feathers. Suds are made in a bowl of lukewarm water and a man's soft shaving brush is used on all parts of the bird's body. Wings and tail feathers are spread out against the side of the bowl and well brushed. Then the bird is given three successive rinses in clear warm water, wrapped in a towel, and placed where it is warm. After most of the moisture has been absorbed from the feathers, the bird is placed in a warm hospital cage or in a warm room and allowed to preen and fluff out its feathers. It should be strictly guarded against drafts, and the cage should be very clean.

Exhibiting budgerigars has its special problems. We have learned that these birds do not go through a regular late summer-early fall molt as do seasonal breeders. The erratic shedding of feathers in these birds at unpredictable times has given showbird breeders many a headache. It happens not infrequently that a bird in perfect show condition drops one of its beautiful throat spots just before being sent to a show or while at a show. Or a long tail feather comes out which leaves the second one unsupported. A bird not in full feather does not win the prize it would otherwise deserve.

To guard against such mishaps, breeders often pull both tail feathers two months before a show. The newly grown tail will then be firm and not drop out. Frayed or defective feathers are also pulled at this time. In the case of throat spots this is a risky procedure because the feather bearing the spot is very small and easily breaks off. It will not regrow before show time. Most breeders, therefore, leave matters to luck and hope for the best. (Those who do not wish to take a chance may take a pair of tweezers and carefully pull the spot feathers four weeks before the show, being sure to take hold of the feather close to the skin.) Another risk which besets the exhibitor is the possibility that a prospective show bird will go into a complete molt losing many breast feathers. Nothing can be done in such a case except substituting another bird. This is the reason budgerigar breeders always train and prepare more birds for a show than they intend to send.

The novice often feels uncertain as to which of his birds he should select for exhibition. It must be remembered that the budgerigar is a type bird which means that the judges place the highest awards on those birds which are of a streamlined shape, tapering evenly from head to tip of tail without marked breaks. The wings should not cross above the tail. The head should be large and well rounded, and the neck thick. The bib should not be short and the spots should be of pleasing size in those varieties which carry spots.

Body size plays an important role in show specimens. Large birds are harder to produce than small ones and will win over a small bird when other points are equal. However, large specimens are not good show birds if out of proportion, clumsy looking, not streamlined, or with feathers which are too long and coarse and are worn loosely instead of tightly to the body. Bulges of fat detract from the beauty of a show bird, as well as thinness. For additional information on the art of exhibiting and judging we should like to recommend the writings of W. Watmough, an authority on the subject.

Shipping to bird shows is best done in trunks especially constructed for this purpose. Usually four standard show cages fit into one trunk which admits light through windows made of shatter-proof material. One bird is placed in each show cage and labeled according to directions given by the show committee. If the show cages are of the box-type, holes for ventilation may be drilled into the side wall of the trunk at either end. A slight cross-current of air will not injure the birds in this instance, because the holes are small and the birds are protected by the solid walls of their cages.

Index